W9-CGT-755

ENVIRONMENTAL POLICIES IN TURKEY

ORGANISATION FOR ECONOMIC CO-OPERATION AND DEVELOPMENT

ANP2725-0/1

ORGANISATION FOR ECONOMIC CO-OPERATION
AND DEVELOPMENT

Pursuant to Article 1 of the Convention signed in Paris on 14th December 1960, and which came into force on 30th September 1961, the Organisation for Economic Co-operation and Development (OECD) shall promote policies designed:

— to achieve the highest sustainable economic growth and employment and a rising standard of living in Member countries, while maintaining financial stability, and thus to contribute to the development of the world economy;

— to contribute to sound economic expansion in Member as well as non-member countries in the process of economic development; and

— to contribute to the expansion of world trade on a multilateral, non-discriminatory basis in accordance with international obligations.

The original Member countries of the OECD are Austria, Belgium, Canada, Denmark, France, Germany, Greece, Iceland, Ireland, Italy, Luxembourg, the Netherlands, Norway, Portugal, Spain, Sweden, Switzerland, Turkey, the United Kingdom and the United States. The following countries became Members subsequently through accession at the dates indicated hereafter: Japan (28th April 1964), Finland (28th January 1969), Australia (7th June 1971) and New Zealand (29th May 1973). The Commission of the European Communities takes part in the work of the OECD (Article 13 of the OECD Convention). Yugoslavia has a special status at OECD (agreement of 28th October 1961).

Publié en français sous le titre :

**POLITIQUES DE
L'ENVIRONNEMENT EN TURQUIE**

PREFACE

This review of Turkey's environmental policies is the seventh one of its type to be conducted by the OECD, following similar reviews of environmental policies in Sweden, Japan, New Zealand, Greece, Yugoslavia and Finland. As was the case with the previous studies, the review was undertaken at the request of the Government of the reviewed country.

This review was prepared by the OECD Secretariat with the assistance of experts provided by Australia, Canada, Finland, Italy, the Netherlands, New Zealand, United States and Yugoslavia.

The report and its conclusions build upon material provided by the Turkish authorities in a document entitled "Selected Environmental Topics"; data and views gathered by the OECD expert team during the fact-finding mission of June 1991, as well as during additional ad hoc missions to Turkey by OECD staff members and consultants; and two consultation and review meetings which took place in Ankara and in Paris.

The purpose of the Ankara consultation meeting in March 1992 was to obtain further information and views from those concerned with environmental matters in Turkey; detailed discussions took place with representatives of the government, senior officials of the departments and agencies responsible for environmental management as well as members of other departments.

The purpose of the Paris review meeting in April 1992 was to further assess within the OECD Environment Committee the ways and means to better integrate environmental protection within economic development and to strengthen the implementation of environmental policies in Turkey. The Delegation of Turkey was conducted by Mr. D. Akyürek, Environment Minister, and included high level representatives of the Ministry of Foreign Affairs, Ministry of Finance and customs, Ministry of Public Works, State Planning Organisation and Turkish Water Resources Agency.

Subsequently, the OECD Council agreed to derestrict the assessment report and its conclusions and the Secretary-General agreed that the review should be published on his responsibility.

The OECD is greatly indebted to the Government of Turkey for making this Review possible and for providing the information on which it is based.

ALSO AVAILABLE

OECD Environmental Data : Compendium 1991 (1991)
(97 91 06 3) ISBN 92-64-03512-5   FF235   £33.00   US$56.00   DM97

The State of the Environment. With Free Supplement: Environmental Indicators. A Preliminary Set (1991)
(97 91 01 1) ISBN 92-64-13442-5   FF180   £22.00   US$38.00   DM70

Transport and the Environment (1988)
(97 88 01 1) ISBN 92-64-13045-4   FF95   £11.20   US$21.00   DM41

DETAILED TABLE OF CONTENTS

LIST OF FIGURES AND TABLES

LIST OF INSETS

Chapter 1

THE CONTEXT OF ENVIRONMENTAL POLICIES

I.   PHYSICAL CONTEXT

Extending from Europe to Asia over the Dardanelles and Bosphorus straits, allowing a natural connection between the basins of the Mediterranean and Black seas, Turkey is on the crossroads linking Asia, Europe and Africa; 97 per cent of its total area (777 971 km2) is situated in Asia.

Four seas surround the country; the total coastlines amount to 8 272 km (including the shores of the Sea of Marmara). The Aegean and Mediterranean shorelines exceed 4 500 km; Turkey shares the shores of the Black Sea (1 700 km) with Bulgaria, Romania and states of the ex-Soviet Union. These coastal areas provide Turkey with major environmental assets, including the absorbing capacity of coastal waters. At the same time Turkey also has a responsibility to develop these areas in a sustainable way.

Because of varied geographical conditions, Turkey shows great diversity in geological structure, topography, climate and plant cover. The country is usually subdivided into seven regions: four of them (Black Sea, Marmara, Aegean, Mediterranean) are coastal units, and the remaining three (Central Anatolia, East Anatolia, Southeast Anatolia) are mountainous and subject to harsh climatic conditions (either dry or cold). (Figure 1)

A third of the total land area is estimated to be suitable for various types of agriculture. The topography is generally sloping highland or mountainous, even in coastal areas; only 10 per cent of the country lies below 250m above sea level. The average altitude in the country is 1250m: high mountains are concentrated in Central and Eastern Anatolia. Owing to this tormented relief, 62.5 per cent of the land has slopes steeper than 15 per cent. All of these aspects have repercussions on agricultural techniques and soil erosion.

11

Figure 1. GEOGRAPHICAL REGIONS OF TURKEY

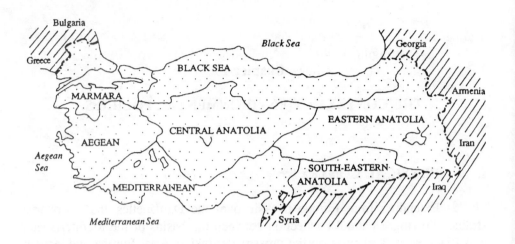

Turkey also shows great variety in climate. The western part is mostly of a Mediterranean type: summers are long, warm and dry, winters are mild and wetter. Annual average temperatures vary between 18-20°C on the south coast and fall to 14-15°C on the west coast. Following the same north-south pattern, rainfall is more abundant in the Marmara area than in the Aegean and Mediterranean regions. In the heart of Central Anatolia, Turkey's driest region, annual average rainfall is very low (250-350 mm/yr): salt lakes occur and water shortages as well as wind erosion appear to be limitative factors for agricultural production. On the northern coasts of the Black Sea region, rainy summers allow the cultivation of tea and nuts; but heavy rainfall also contributes to the generation of multiple natural hazards (e.g., landslides, floods).

In the interior areas towards the east, continental conditions and high mountains are causes of cold and snowy winters with temperatures fluctuating between -10°C and 0°C; in the low lands (Diyarbakir region), the summers are warm and dry. These eastern mountains may be considered the "water towers" of the Middle East. Two major rivers, the Euphrates and the Tigris, whose waters flow through Syria and Iraq down to Mesopotamia and the Persian Gulf, rise there. The variety in geography and climate also creates a great variety of natural resources and environmental conditions. Environmental policy has to deal with these variations and adapt to the great regional differences.

Turkey has high seismic activity. Numerous earthquakes, some quite destructive, occur mostly along the North-Anatolian fault-line running from the Dardanelles Strait through the Pontus mountains, in a line parallel to the Black Sea coast. The fragility of these regions creates specific environmental problems. Industrial plants, storage facilities and environmental infrastructure require special construction to withstand earthquakes.

II.   HUMAN CONTEXT

1.   *The highest population growth rate in OECD*

In 1927, the population of Turkey was approximately 13.7 million. Today, it has reached 56 million. In the past several decades, the annual population growth rate has never fallen below 2 per cent except during the period between the years 1935-45 (2.2 per cent, i.e. 1.3 million, between 1989 and 1990). According to UN population growth projections, the total population of Turkey is expected to reach 65 million in 2000 and 92 million in 2025. This growth rate is the highest of all OECD Member countries. From 1970 to 1990, mean population change in OECD was 16.2 per cent while reaching 56.2 per cent in Turkey. Nevertheless the population density of the country (72 inh./km2) remains one of the lowest in Europe, similar to that of Spain (78 inh./km2).

2.   *Rural migration: a constant and increasing trend*

High population growth leads to high migration rates towards both internal destinations (mostly the largest Turkish towns) and foreign countries (mostly in Western Europe). More than 6 per cent of the Turkish population (around 3.5 million people) lives in foreign countries, mainly in Germany (about 2.8 million), France, Belgium and Austria; once peasants, these migrants usually work in the industrial sector. Inside Turkey, industrial towns are the most attractive to rural migrants, especially when industry grows together with harbour activities, as in Ìstanbul, Ìzmit, Ìzmir, Adana, Mersin, Ìskenderun and Samsun.

The current accelerated migration movements from rural areas to urban centres reflect recent and profound changes in the agricultural sector, where mechanisation and the transfer of land uses have led to more intense cultivation practices on pastures and grasslands previously devoted to extensive animal husbandry. These changes have also led to modifications in the social structure of Turkey's rural and urban communities. The intensification and mechanisation of agriculture and the transfer of rich agricultural land for urban uses led to perilous environmental impacts in certain areas. These impacts included salinisation, soil erosion, and pollution of surface waters and aquifers.

3. *Urban centres of various sizes*

Turkey is administratively divided into 73 provinces and 829 districts. In 1990 41 per cent of the population was living in rural areas, and this share is quickly diminishing.

The 1985 census counts 640 cities (> 2000 inhabitants) grouping 26.5 million people. The 53 largest cities (>100 000 inhabitants) concentrate more than 16 million people (i.e., one-third of the total population and 62 per cent of the urban population of Turkey). Another group of 148 towns (from 20 000 to 100 000 inhabitants) corresponds to 23.2 per cent of the total urban population. These cities and towns are distributed all over the country, but trends show a concentration of migrant population in the coastal areas and in the capital city, Ankara.

In recent decades, the biggest cities (İstanbul, Ankara and İzmir) have grown so fast that imbalances have appeared in the urban network of the country. At the same time, while some of the regional capitals (Konya, Diyarbakir, Samsun, Trabzon) still offer an attractive employment capacity, the more traditionally trade-oriented cities (e.g. Afyon, Aydin, Bolu, Burdur, Erzurum, Kars, Sinop, Van) show signs of a slowdown, sometimes leading to the departure of their inhabitants.

The size of the country, the growth of the population and the drift to the cities not only create environmental problems but also pose major challenges to the administrative make-up and capacity of governmental authorities at central, provincial and municipal levels.

4. *Growth of cities*

Turkey's population is growing fast, but its cities grow even faster. The annual increase of the urban population between 1985 and 1990 was between 4 and 5 per cent in 18 of the 73 provinces and exceeded 5 per cent in eight of them. The percentage is about the same if the city centre itself is considered.

The share of urban population, which was only 24.2 per cent in 1927 and 38.4 per cent in 1970, reached 59 per cent in 1990. But this urban population is concentrated in the three largest urban areas: İstanbul, Ankara and İzmir. These three provinces account for 23 per cent of the total population and 35 per cent of the total urban population.

Rapid expansion of towns has engulfed fertile agricultural land and has caused complex environmental problems in the towns. The inadequacy of infrastructure, public services, energy distribution, water and sewerage networks, urban transport, housing, green spaces, etc. is increasing.

5. *Environmental awareness of the urban population*

Concern for the environment has grown considerably in recent years in Turkey. The mass media have reflected this growing interest which also appears to be very strong at the local level and in the rural communities. On the other hand people comprising the rural influx to towns care less about their new environment. In cities, it is chiefly the people who have lived there for at least one generation who feel more concerned about the quality of air, water, landscape and urbanism. Yet quality of life is slowly becoming a political issue.

III. ECONOMIC CONTEXT

1. *The liberalisation of the economy*

Since 1980, Turkey has launched an ambitious market-oriented development programme, which puts a strong emphasis on the integration of industry in international markets by shifting from import-substitution to export-oriented industry. The trade balance in low-technology goods swung rapidly from deficit into a sizeable surplus. Deterioration of the trade balance in high and medium-technology goods is becoming less pronounced.

2. *A very high economic growth rate*

This high economic growth rate is evident in all sectors of the economy and consequently accompanied by the increase in polluting activities in commerce, agriculture, transport and energy production and use.

From 1980 to 1989, average annual growth of GDP was 5.3 per cent compared with the OECD average of 3.0 per cent. The OECD projection is for a slowdown of economic growth to 3.5 per cent in 1991, after an estimated rise of activity of 7.5 per cent in 1990. (Table 1)

Table 1. **GDP, 1980-1990**

	GDP *a)* (billion US$)	Change in GDP *b)* (%)		GDP per capita *a)* (US$/cap)
	1990	1980-90	1989-90	1990
Turkey	161.3	5.36	9.19	2 857
Canada	433.2	2.98	0.42	16 285
U.S.A.	4 589.8	2.95	0.92	18 250
France	837.2	2.22	2.58	14 837
Italy	984.5	2.08	4.72	15 147 *c)*
w. Germany	786.1	2.21	1.95	13 807
Spain	391.0	2.93	3.61	10 037

a)   at price levels and purchasing power parities of 1985
b)   average annual volume change in GDP
c)   1989 data

Source: OECD.

3.   *Rising industrial production and exports*

Due to the successful implementation of outward-oriented economic policies, exports have tripled since 1980 and the export target for 1987 was surpassed. The value of Turkey's exports increased from $3 billion in 1980 to $12 billion in 1989; the export/import ratio rose from 40 per cent in 1980 to 74 per cent in 1989. Industrial exports (in $ terms) have grown at an annual rate of 20 per cent. Exports of manufactured products today account for about 80 per cent of Turkish exports, compared with only one-third at the beginning of the

16

decade. Sustained also by increasing exports of agricultural products, the volume of Turkish foreign trade has thus shown a substantial rise.

In 1989, 78.6 per cent of Turkey's exports were industrial products, compared to 64 per cent in 1983. Germany is Turkey's biggest single country market, followed by France and the United States. Turkey also conducts a substantial share of its trade with Middle East countries and North Africa.

4. *Deterioration of the balance of payments and external debt*

Although increased merchandise exports have helped to improve Turkey's balance of payments, the import of consumer goods has grown dramatically in the last ten years, so that the balance of payments shows an increasing deterioration.

In 1990, the trade deficit, which had fallen substantially in 1988 to $1.8 billion, appears to have increased to more than $9 billion, largely due to the economic consequences of the Gulf crisis. Net tourism revenus and remittances from abroad are strong positive forces. The trade deficit and growing external debt were prohibiting factors in obtaining additional funds for environmental investment from the international capital market.

Between 1984 and 1987, the stock of total disbursed external debt doubled to $40.2 billion. Since then, the growth of foreign debt has slowed substantially. By the end of 1990, it may have reached $45 billion; 40 per cent of the government's budget outlay is devoted to debt servicing.

5. *A high inflation rate and increasing government budget deficits*

Inflation remains the greatest challenge for Turkish economic policy. The average annual rate roughly doubled in 1988 compared with the year before, staying out of range of any inflation rates observed in other OECD Member countries. In 1990 consumer prices increased by 60 per cent. Public sector borrowing requirements continue to rise steadily. In fact much of the price rise can be linked with government budget deficits. Moreover, as a share of GNP, the Turkish public sector is the smallest in the OECD, and the amount of publicly provided services is often regarded as inadequate.

6. *Unemployment*

With an official rate of 10.4 per cent of the labour force, unemployment in Turkey is among the highest of the OECD countries. The real figure is clearly higher since many unemployed workers are not registered because of the absence of any unemployment insurance. Seasonal unemployment in rural areas is not taken into account, and the female labour force is clearly underestimated.

A large percentage of the population still makes its living from farming and animal husbandry. In parallel, the services sector has been growing fast in terms of share of the total labour force (from 20 per cent in 1965 to 36 per cent in 1988).

The high levels of unemployment and underemployment also affect environmental policies. Environmental policies can be used to create employment without putting extra strain on resources. However, old factories cannot be closed on environmental grounds because such closures could lead to unemployment in critical areas.

7. *State enterprise sector (SES)*

The existence and weight of the SES's enterprises in Turkey are of great importance with regard to environmental performance. Turkey's biggest plants (iron, steel, cement, chemicals, paper, textile, foodstuffs, etc.) are state-owned. Thus the state is to be considered responsible for their environmental impacts and management issues.

Reform of the SES was one of the major objectives of the Turkish structural adjustment of 1980. Ever since, policy initiatives have aimed at freeing the state enterprises from direct government intervention in their price setting, investment and employment decisions. Nevertheless, the State enterprises have remained directly attached to specific State Ministers, who are still responsible for their management.

State enterprises are a particular problem for the environment. Often they are old, inefficient and polluting. Municipal authorities find it difficult to impose environmental measures on these enterprises as they are protected, for employment reasons, by the central authorities.

IV.   ENERGY CONTEXT

1.   *Production and growing requirements*

Energy produced in Turkey has increased from 6.4 million TOE in 1950 to 25.1 million TOE in 1990; in parallel, primary energy consumption values have risen from 6.9 million TOE in 1950 to 51.6 million TOE in 1990. Turkey's energy needs (1990) are met by oil (45.5 per cent), coal, lignite and asphaltite (29.8 per cent), non-commercial fuels (woods, dung and plant wastes: 15.3 per cent), water resources (4.0 per cent) and natural gas (5.5 per cent).

Since the production is not sufficient to meet the actual demand values, 54 per cent of Turkey's total consumed energy was imported in 1990, with oil accounting for 75 per cent of these imports. Recently, in addition to low-sulphur coal and electricity, both since 1973, imports of natural gas (since 1987) have been rapidly growing.

2.   *Energy consumption: domestic lignites and imported oil*

As shown by the sources of the energy produced and consumed in Turkey, several air pollution problems may arise from the overall uses of lignites and oil. (Figure 2) However, due to the high ash and sulphur content of the Turkish lignites, a certain amount of low-sulphur hard coal is being imported for the cities with air pollution problems. In recent years, a development programme based on the importation of gas has also started to replace the use of this lignite in house-heating. In parallel, with financial assistance from the World Bank, rehabilitation studies are being undertaken in the Zonguldak hard coal basin.

Oil represents about 45.5 per cent of the actual energy requirements of Turkey, against 61.1 per cent in 1970. But in 1990 it generated only 6.9 per cent of the power generated in the country (against 17.7 per cent for natural gas, for example). This means that it is mainly the transportation sector which now depends on oil energy. Turkey's actual reserves of recoverable oil are now estimated to be about 20.8 million tonnes, of which 99.4 per cent is located in Southeastern Anatolia. Turkey's crude oil production amounts to 3.8 million t/y, an amount which is far too inadequate to cover oil consumption, which reached 23.5 million t/y in 1989 and 1990 (data show a 56 per cent growth in oil consumption between 1979 and 1990).

Energy consumption has grown more since 1973 than in any other OECD country, but per capita energy consumption remains the lowest. Energy

Figure 2. ENERGY SUPPLY, 1970-1989

TOTAL ENERGY SUPPLY, BY SOURCE

Situation in 1989

	Turkey	Canada	USA	France	w. Germany	Italy	Spain	OECD	
Total	48.9	219.7	1945.5	218.1	271.6	153.5	86.4	3988.7	Mtoe
per unit GDP	0.76	0.55	0.43	0.37	0.40	0.32	0.43	0.40	Toe/1000 US$
per capita	0.88	8.37	7.82	3.88	4.38	2.67	2.22	4.80	Toe/cap.

Trends 1970-1989

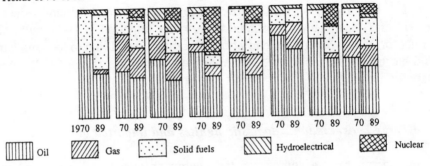

1970 89 70 89 70 89 70 89 70 89 70 89 70 89 70 89

Oil Gas Solid fuels Hydroelectrical Nuclear

ENERGY INTENSITY *

Index 1980=100

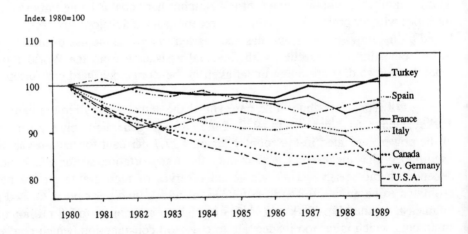

* Total primary energy supply per unit of GDP in terms of tonnes of oil equivalent per 1000 US$ (at 1985 prices and exchange rates).

Source: OECD-IEA

20

consumption is highest in the residential sector, as a result of demographic growth and of housing improvements. It is to supply this demand that gas and coal are being imported, as well as to reduce the environmental impact of the use of home-produced lignites in heating urban dwellings. However, consumption trends over the last 20 years show that the domestic share decreases as the share of industry and agriculture increases, which means that other policies will be needed to reduce emissions linked to the energy production sector (i.e., thermal power plants, transportation sector, industrial emissions).

3. *Oil imports being replaced by electricity*

Hydropower contributes 40 per cent of the total electricity produced by power plants in Turkey. However, its share in power generation dropped from 48.8 per cent in 1980 to 40 per cent in 1990; this decrease is concomitant with an increase in the share of natural gas.

Turkey, with its pronounced relief and small mountainous basins, possesses a great capacity for the production of hydroelectricity. However, most of the actual or potential sites are located in the eastern part of the country. Since the demand is mostly situated in the western part of the country the transfer of electricity will be an increasingly urgent problem. To encourage economic development, industrial electricity tariffs vary among regions: they are 5 per cent below average in 32 provinces in eastern Turkey and 15 per cent above average in the west.

4. *Energy use: trends show growing rates of intensity and waste*

Turkey's energy requirements appear to be low when measured by per capita ratios: 0.9 TOE/cap. in 1989, while the average for the OECD Member countries is 4.8 TOE/cap. But two other indicators show inefficiency in energy use, which leads to waste of energy:

--   the total energy requirements by unit of GDP are 0.8 TOE/$1 000 (1989) although the OECD average is only 0.4 TOE/$1 000. This means that Turkey uses more energy for production than any other OECD Member country;

--   trends also show that energy intensity is declining in all OECD Member countries except Turkey, where it is growing. The ratio for energy requirements grew by 52 per cent in Turkey from 1970 to 1990, while decreasing by 26 per cent during the same period in the OECD area.

Since more than half (54 per cent) of Turkey's energy requirements are met by imports and are expected to grow very fast in the near future, it appears necessary to follow energy saving policies and to use more adapted technologies, which would benefit both the economy and the environment.

5.   *High demand for fuelwood*

Turkish forests are being over-exploited for the supply of fuelwood: although their potential energy production is estimated to be approximately 8.5 million tonnes, production in recent years stood around 18 million tonnes. The idea of switching to "energy forests" in order to prevent the illegal cutting of forests for fuelwood and their consecutive destruction has been endorsed by the Ministry of Energy and Natural Resources. These energy forests would be composed of rapidly growing trees developed exclusively for the purpose of energy.

6.   *Renewable sources of energy*

As a result of low income and inadequate fuel supply in rural areas, **animal wastes** are used as fuels in some parts of Turkey today. Furthermore, **plant wastes** such as hazelnut and walnut shells, olive pulp, cotton seeds, sunflower seed hulls and corncobs are also burned for heating purposes. The share of such wastes in total energy production is 6 per cent. Manure supplies 9 per cent of the country's energy needs.

The potential **geothermal** electrical power production has been estimated to be 4500 MW, with a thermal capacity of 31 100 MW, suitable for city and greenhouse heating. Geothermal production in Turkey has started with the construction of a power plant, with the assistance of an Italian firm, at Denizli-Kizildere in the Aegean region. This is a typical field for bilateral co-operation and technology transfer, as has been shown by projects for other plants:

--   a second plant is being constructed in collaboration with Iceland;

--   a project in association with Japan is underway for Aydin-Germancik (Aegean region);

--   French firms have started research on the exploitation of fields at Canakkale-Tuzla (near the Dardanelles strait).

Solar energy is widely used for water-heating purposes in most cities situated along the Mediterranean and Aegean coasts where water-heater reservoirs on every roof are very noticeable. Turkey possesses significant solar energy potential, which has been estimated to be 26 million TOE thermal and 8.8 million TOE electrical.

V.   INSTITUTIONAL CONTEXT

1.   *The state: strong political and administrative centralisation*

A democratic and secular state

The Republic of Turkey is a democratic and secular state. The President of the Republic is the head of State. He represents the Republic of Turkey and the unity of the Turkish nation, and ensures the implementation of the Constitution and the regular and harmonious functioning of the organs of the State. The President is elected by the Assembly. Presidential elections were most recently held by the Assembly in 1989 and occur every seven years.

The Prime Minister is selected from the members of the Grand National Assembly of Turkey and appointed by the President of the Republic; the Ministers, who are not required to be deputies, are selected by the Prime Minister and appointed by the President.

The power to legislate is vested in the Turkish Grand National Assembly which exercises its parliamentary control functions by means of parliamentary questions, parliamentary investigations, general debates, ministerial questioning and inquiries. Legislative power cannot be delegated. The 450 members of the Assembly are elected by the nation every five years. The political system is of a multi-party type. Legislative elections were last held in November 1991.

The local authorities: Governors (appointed) and Mayors (elected)

There are 73 appointed governors, all affiliated with the Ministry of the Interior. The Governor is the head of the provincial local government and its chief executive. Governors usually act in line with the decisions made by the

23

provincial general assembly, which consists of members elected by the proportional representation system for a four-year term.

Provincial Special Administrations, municipalities and villages are the three types of local administration operating in Turkey; most important are the municipalities, set up in all provinces and some other comparatively heavily populated centres. The municipal administration is comprised of an assembly (elected by popular vote every five years), a council (elected by the proportional representation system) and a mayor, elected for a five-year term.

2.   *Environmental institutions*

Numerous laws

The Environment Law which came into force in 1983 endorses the Polluter-Pays Principle and handles environmental issues on a very broad scope. The aim of the Law, which considers the environment as a whole, is not only to prevent and eliminate environmental pollution, but also to allow for the management of the natural and historical values and the land in such a way as to utilise and preserve its richness for future generations. According to the basic principles that govern the application of the Environmental Law, and as stated in the Constitution, citizens as well as the state bear responsibility for the protection of the environment. Also stated in the Law is the principle that in economic activities, when determining production methods, every effort should be made to minimise and solve environmental problems.

Complementary to the Environment Law and its regulations, other laws govern the protection/conservation of the environment, the prevention/control of pollution, and the implementation of measures for the prevention of pollution:

--   Water Products: Law and Regulations (1971-1973);

--   Tourism Incentive Law (1982);

--   National Parks Law (1983);

--   Conservation of Cultural and Natural Assets Law (1983);

--   Specially Protected Areas (1969 Decree having force of law);

--   The Coast Law (1990), etc.

24

In line with the Environmental Law, several regulations have been published since 1983:

-- Regulation of Pollution Prevention Fund (1985);

-- Regulation of Air Quality Control (1986);

-- Regulation of Noise Control (1986);

-- Regulation of the Penalties to be Imposed on Ships and other Sea Vessels, Procedures for Collecting Fines and Receipts (1987);

-- Regulation of Water Pollution Control (1988);

-- Regulation of the Control of Solid Wastes (1991).

The following additional regulations are under preparation:

-- Environmental Impact Assessment Statements (EIAs). The lack of such a regulation at this time makes it difficult to enforce controls which could prevent several types of degradation;

-- Hazardous Wastes and Chemical Substances. This regulation will be closely related to the international legislation (the Basel Convention) since Turkey is very sensitive to the problem of illegal waste imports.

Finally, two important laws govern relationships between central authorities with municipalities: laws 3030 and 3194.

Recent creation of the Ministry of Environment

Since 1978, the "Prime Ministry Undersecretariat for Environment" attached to an unspecified "Ministry of State" was responsible for the co-ordination of all national and international activities pertaining to the environment. This co-ordination between all the other Administrations involved in the protection of the environment, the prevention and reduction of pollutions, etc. was the main task of these services. The Undersecretariat was the institution expected to set environmental policy, to co-ordinate and prepare regulations, and to co-operate with other ministries and agencies as required to ensure sound environmental management.

In August 1991, the Undersecretariat for the Environment was promoted to the rank of Ministry of Environment. This change may lead to a diversification of its responsibilities, to an expansion of its personnel and perhaps will empower this Administration with some right to intervene, to control and to implement policies adapted for the protection and conservation of the environment and for the sustainable development and management of natural resources.

Other bodies involved in environmental protection and management

Attached to the new Ministry are several bodies whose functions remain to be defined: the Supreme Environmental Board, Environment Council and the Local Environmental Boards. A more recent (1989) organisation, the Directorate for Specially Protected Areas, which was dependent on the Prime Minister and the Undersecretariat and now is affiliated with the Ministry of Environment, has responsibility for protecting the environment in the "Specially Protected Areas". This designation refers to agreements between the Turkish Government and the UNEP Mediterranean Action Plan in Athens.

Moreover, in the spring of 1991, 23 provincial and local environmental foundations were created on a semi-voluntary and semi-governmental basis for the discussion of environmental matters with the Boards. The creation of these foundations ensures that problems are now channeled to the responsible regional and central agencies.

The **General Directorate of State Hydraulic Works (SHW) and the Bank of Provinces** are affiliations of the **Ministry of Public Works and Settlement**. Besides the development of hydraulic resources for irrigation and hydropower, the SHW is responsible for the prevention of damage to surface and ground waters and for the quality of these waters depending on their uses. In cities with fewer than 100 000 inhabitants, SHW ensures the long-term supply of drinking, utility and industrial water. The Bank of Provinces is responsible for planning sewerage and wastewater treatment plants in cities with fewer than 100 000 inhabitants. This organisation supplies financing and credit as well as technical assistance to the municipalities for infrastructural projects connected with the sanitation services and drinking water supply for population centres other than the major cities.

The Ministry of Energy and Natural Resources is responsible for the production and control of sustainable consumption of natural resources and energy, as well as for investigations of river discharges.

The **Ministry of Industry and Trade** is the responsible authority for consultancy on industrial matters and for the development of industrial policy, including those policies concerning the environment.

Within the **Ministry of Agriculture and Rural Affairs, the General Directorate of Protection and Control, the General Directorate of Forestry and the General Directorate of Rural Services** also conducts projects related to environmental management: sewage systems and irrigation networks in rural areas.

Within the Ministry of Forestry the General Directorate of Protection and Control and the General Directorate of Forestry conduct projects related to water pollution control; identification, protection and management of national parks, nature reserves, nature parks, etc.

The **Environmental Health Service** of the Ministry of Health is responsible for health networks and, in particular, for the monitoring of air quality (measures of SO_2 and PM concentrations).

The **State Planning Organisation** attached to the Prime Ministry is the main body responsible for the preparation of five-year plans and for annual implementation programmes in all sectors of activity. Recently, this agency carried out the installation, accounting and survey for the development of environmental statistics. Its role might actually evolve towards a consultative-type function attached to the central government (Prime Minister's Office).

3.   *International relations*

An integral part of the international scene

The international legislation to which Turkey adheres and organisations to which Turkey belongs -- such as the United Nations system, NATO (1952), the OECD, the Council of Europe (1949) -- influence the definition of national policies and the decision processes in the country. Turkey, an associate member of the EEC since the Ankara agreement of 12 September 1963, officially applied for full membership in 1987.

Turkey is also at the crossroads of the Near and Middle-East countries. It shares long borders with Syria, Iraq, Iran and the former USSR (Commonwealth of Independent States). Since the 18th century, the trade roads and major transport lanes have changed; but Turkey, as a secular state, can still play the "buffer" and "liaison" role between Europe and the Middle East.

Involvement in international aspects of environmental affairs

Turkey takes part in various conventions, treaties, agreements and protocols. Turkey has been a member of the Barcelona Convention since 1976 and thus participates in the implementation of the UNEP Mediterranean Action Plan, along with the 16 other Member countries. It has also ratified the Protocols annexed to the Convention:

--   Protocol for the Protection of the Mediterranean Sea against Dumping from Ships and Aircraft (1976);

--   Protocol concerning Operation in Combating Pollution of the Mediterranean Sea by Oil and Other Harmful Substances in Cases of Emergency (1976);

--   Protocol for the Protection of the Mediterranean Sea against Pollution from Land-based Sources (1980);

--   Protocol on the Mediterranean Specially-Protected Areas (1982).

Turkey also supports studies related to the Genoa Declaration by identifying activities to be undertaken within the framework of the Mediterranean Action Plan. This was approved in 1985 for a ten-year period. Within this framework, Turkey participates in international projects, such as the MED-POL, the Project related to the pollution from land-based sources, Izmir Coastal Area Management Programme and the Iskenderun Bay Project.

Turkey has also signed or ratified the following conventions:

--   Convention on European Wild Life and Their Habitats (Bern 1973): ratified in 1984;

--   Convention on Long Range Trans-boundary Air Pollution (Geneva, 1979) and protocol on financing the EMEP programme;

--   Basel Convention on Hazardous Wastes and Their Traffic: signed in 1989.

Turkey has not yet signed the Convention on Wetlands of International

Importance especially as Waterfowl Habitats (also called the "Ramsar" Convention). It intends to become a party to the Vienna Convention on the Protection of the Ozone Layer and its Montreal Protocol.

Very sensitive to the international dimension of environmental issues, Turkey is currently involved in programmes which necessitate close collaboration and discussion with its neighbours, especially concerning the Black Sea and the use of water resources in the region.

Turkey has been involved in international actions in several fields:

-- the prevention of pollution in the Black Sea. The proceedings started five years ago and were intended to culminate in an international agreement which should soon be completed. Turkey is urgently expected to take positive action to stem the accelerating depletion of fish stock in the Black Sea;

-- water use in the region. One of the dimensions of this problem is related to the international political, economic and ecological significance of the waterworks being realised and planned in watersheds which contribute to the water supply (Tigris and Euphrates rivers) of neighbouring countries;

-- the presence of hazardous wastes, mainly as the result of the dumping of wastes into the Black Sea which also affects the Bosphorus and the Sea of Marmara;

-- air pollution, because of its increasing significance and concomitant health problems in several of the country's major cities.

VI.   NATURAL RESOURCES CONTEXT

1.   *Land use and soils*

Soils of Turkey have been ploughed, and herds have grazed on the Anatolian plateaux for thousands of years. The earliest Neolithic village in the world, Catal Hüyük, is situated on the South edge of the inner plateaux of Anatolia. Numerous sites of villages dating from 9000-8000 years ago have been found in Turkey. And the nearer we come to history, the more villages there are. The sites of some cities have been occupied for 4000 to 5000 years.

Land use - current trends

Current trends are marked by the expansion of agriculture through irrigation and the development of marginal land and by the intensification of pasture on fragile soils whose structure is easily destroyed. The present land use in Turkey is as follows:

Arable and permanent cropland	36.0 %
Pasture	28.0 %
Forests and heath	30.0 %
Marshes, river beds, bare rock	4.0 %
Inland waters	1.3 %
Settlements	0.7 %

The above land use does not always take account of the land use capability as determined in a nationwide classification. About 3.3 million ha out of the 16.7 million ha considered suitable are presently being irrigated. A further 1 million ha will be added before the end of 1994. The GAP project in Southeastern Anatolia will be an important part of this.

Soil pollution - current trends

Agricultural practices, as in other OECD countries, are impacting on soils and water courses through the use of fertilizers and pesticides. The use of fertilizers in kg/ha has increased fourfold since 1970 under the influence of Government incentives, but it is still only about half the OECD average. Similarly, the use of pesticides is increasing rapidly in Turkey. There is a proliferation of active ingredients and of local manufacturing firms. Use has until now concentrated in the Mediterranean region, especially near Adana. Little information is available about pesticide residues in the environment and in humans, but they are likely to be significant. The Government is attempting to achieve better control over the use of pesticides, through, for instance, bans on certain pesticides or information campaigns on the use of pesticides.

Soil degradation - current trends

There is a growing recognition of soil degradation problems in Turkey. About two-thirds of Turkey's land area is subject to moderate to severe water or wind erosion: 500 million tonnes of top soil are lost every year. The intensification of agricultural practices is aggravating the problem. In some areas, e.g. between Ankara and Konya, salinisation is a problem requiring care in the development of irrigation schemes.

Loss of agricultural land through urban expansion - current trends

Agricultural land is being lost in the vicinity of towns through the establishment of squatter settlements, and in the coastal areas through the growth of tourist facilities. As a result of rapid development in Turkey, fertile land is being used more and more for purposes other than agriculture such as housing, industry, and public sector investment. Government policies and loopholes in the law are partly responsible for the unplanned use of farmland for non-agricultural purposes, as taxes, prices and incentives are not harmonized. Improper and unplanned location of sensitive activities also gives rise to soil and water pollution problems.

2. *Forests*

Pressures on forest resources - current trends

Apart from legitimate harvesting, Turkish forests are vulnerable to many uncontrolled uses. The total stock of timber has been declining. Just over one quarter (26.2 per cent) of the surface area of Turkey is covered in forests; almost all are state owned and managed by the General Directorate of Forestry. Turkish forests are made up as follows:

Total forest area of which:	20.2 million ha	
	Production forests	44 %
	Protection forests	2 %
	Degraded forest lands	50 %

The total harvest/annual growth ratio has been calculated at 1.02, i.e. considerably higher than the OECD average. (Figure 3) In addition to **commercial harvesting** and the traditional rights of neighbouring villages to take certain forest products (other than wood), there are significant losses due to illegal cutting and clearing, illegal settlements and pastures, fires and pests. (Figure 4) It is estimated that between 1937 and 1987 the total area of forest cleared for agricultural purposes amounted to 1.2 million ha. The widespread **illegal clearing activities** are partly caused by the confused ownership situation as cadastral surveys for more than half of the total area have yet to be completed. **Fires** are a growing threat especially in the Mediterranean and Aegean areas

31

Figure 3. INTENSITY OF USE OF FOREST

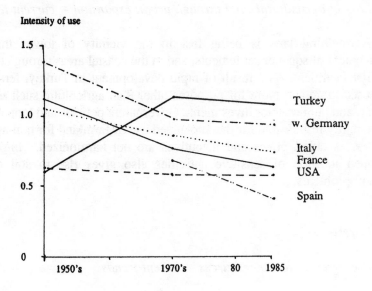

Source : OECD

	Growing stock (m³/ha)	Annual increment (m³/ha)	Annual harvest (Mm³)			Intensity of use (total harvest/annual growth)		
	1980-85	1980-85	1950s	1970s	1980-85	1950s	1970s	1980-85
Turkey	58.0	2.9	7.2	19.9	19.6	0.58	1.04	1.02
Canada	73.4	1.7	71.1	121.4	151.3	..	..	0.47
U.S.A.	109.3	3.6	304.6	397.4	442.7	0.60	0.57	0.58
France	120.0	4.0	35.5	34.7	39.5	1.09	0.75	0.62
w. Germany	224.0	5.7	35.3	33.7	40.5	1.41	0.99	0.96
Italy	154.0	3.1	15.4	11.9	9.0	1.04	0.85	0.75
Spain	68.0	4.3	14.2	16.8	13.3	..	0.66	0.4
OECD	93.2	2.6	703.3	914.3	952.1	..	..	0.52

Source: OECD.

Figure 4. FIREWOOD AND INDUSTRIAL WOOD PRODUCTION, 1938-1987

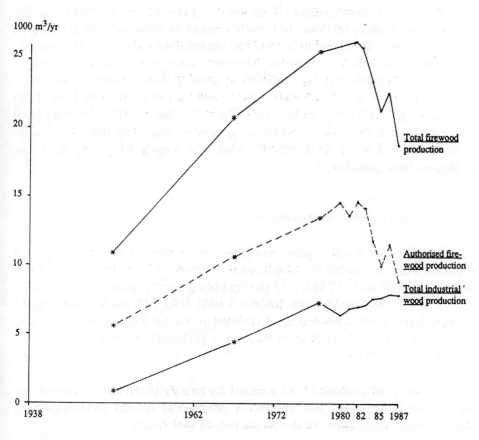

Legend :
* = mean value for periods 1938-62, 1963-72, 1973-82

Source : General Directorate of Forestry, *The Turkish Forestry in the 150th Year of Its Establishment* (1989)

where forest lands are also subject to competitive uses such as urbanisation, tourism, and second homes. With increased cheap imports, harvesting may however decline and help timber use intensity to pass under the sustainable level assuming afforestation at the same time is sufficient.

Afforestation

Planting and management efforts are being carried out in order to fill the supply gap in forestry products, to prevent erosion on slopes and the flooding of the downstream valleys, and to re-establish the natural equilibrium between soil, water and plant cover. Attractive incentives have also been introduced to encourage individuals and legal entities to develop forests either within State forests or on their private grounds. New planting has been carried out at an accelerating pace over the last ten years (Table 2). Some difficulties have been encountered with the lack of technical guidelines regarding purpose, timing, location and extent of these efforts, while the supply of young trees has sometimes been insufficient.

Other environmental dimensions

The Turkish forest regime recognises the statutes for various types of protected areas and allows their application to forests. The 45 **protected forests** cover a total area of 387 238 ha, 70 per cent being located within national parks. Forests under such statutes are protected until they become logging forests. Logging, hunting and pasturing are prohibited over some 8 500 ha located within natural parks. No activity at all is allowed in biogenetic reserves where forests cover some 20 000 ha.

To solve the problem of the demand for **energy** (firewood) in rural areas, the Turkish Government has initiated a programme for the development of planted forests designated for the production of fuel wood.

Due to the loss of pastures, especially in the low lands where cultivation is spreading, herds are brought into forested areas where their grazing contributes to the degradation of forests. The management of forested areas in "**grazing forests**" is envisaged and has started to develop.

In the combat against **harmful insects** in forest areas, chemical and mechanical methods have been implemented over 232 434 ha. In consideration of the adverse effects of chemicals on the flora and fauna and because of

Table 2. AFFORESTATION, EROSION CONTROL, IMPROVEMENT OF PASTURES AND ENERGY FOREST ACTIVITIES

Years	Afforestation within forest (hectares)	Afforestation outside forest (hectares)	Erosion control (hectares)	Improvement of pastures (hectares)	Artificial regeneration (hectares)	Energy forest facility (hectares)	Energy forestry renewal (hectares)	Total (hectares)
Start until end of 1982	644 269	26 410	125 424	40 843	255 990	28 204	17 541	1 138 681
1983	63 785	2 425	13 635	3 915	21 450	19 552	7 234	131 996
1984	85 471	2 156	12 608	1 838	17 776	33 602	7 157	160 608
1985	98 198	2 211	15 907	3 395	17 342	46 793	8 813	192 659
1986	106 875	1 834	12 080	2 189	19 840	54 956	10 538	208 312
1987	111 057	2 987	13 964	2 460	23 668	60 352	19 258	233 746
1988	114 898	4 671	23 806	3 640	24 246	61 600	16 790	249 651
Total	1 224 553	42 694	217 424	58 280	380 312	305 059	87 331	2 315 653

Source: *The Turkish Forestry in the 150th year of its establishment* (Ankara / 1989).

environmental pollution issues, biological methods are being used over 60 000 ha.

3. *Pastures and grasslands*

There is a decline in the quantity and quality of pastoral land in Turkey. A traditional part of society is disappearing. Environmental problems are emerging.

The pastures and grasslands are important because they are used as grazing grounds for animal husbandry which provides one-third of the total value of the agricultural production of Turkey and is thus a basic agricultural activity. There are profound linkages between the environmental, social, economic, cultural and political aspects of pastoral agriculture in Turkey. Pastures and grasslands cover 28 per cent or 21.7 million ha of the national territory; most of them can be found in Central, Eastern and South-Eastern Anatolia.

Population growth and the mechanisation of agriculture after World War II caused the progressive clearing of grasslands and forests for farming. In 1954, the total area of pasture and grassland was nearly double what it is today. At the same time there has been a trend towards increased production from the declining areas, causing an intensification of the pressures on pastoral lands:

	1950s	1980s
Area of pasture in million ha	37.8	21.7
No. of cattle units (in millions)	21.0	28.6
Ha/cattle unit	1.8	0.86

It has become a common practice to extend the grazing period by three months both at the beginning and at the end, so that grazing starts when the pasture vegetation has just started to grow and continues until snow falls. Such overgrazing is one of the primary reasons for the actual deterioration of pastures. While grass yield and quality in pastures have declined due to overgrazing, the number of species of pasture vegetation decreased from around 26 to only 5 or 6. The disappearance, either because of overgrazing or of clearance, of local steppe species once present in these pastures, has led to the disappearance of the locally adapted wild fauna.

36

4. *Wetlands*

Turkey is rich in all kinds of virgin wetlands and ranks first in this respect among the European OECD countries; it is also on a vital route for migratory birds.

Some 75 per cent of its 250 wetlands are larger than 100 ha. Because of the wide variety of bird species, especially migratory, to which they provide shelter, some 1.343 million ha of wetlands are considered to be of international importance (Figure 5).

Sixty per cent of the marshes are freshwater ecosystems; 20 per cent are saltwater; 70 per cent of the Turkish wetlands are less than six metres deep. Exposed to sunlight, they act as refuges and food reserves for aquatic birds.

Anatolia is crossed by two major bird migration routes. Of the nearly 400 species of birds found in Turkey, 250 are migratory birds. Approximately one-third of the 110 species that migrate to Turkey in summer brood and find refuge in Turkey. The winter migratory birds also use Turkey's wetlands as their stop-over.

5. *Flora and fauna*

Turkey's unique flora - current trends

The wealth of Turkey's endemic plant species makes it one of the world's most important countries in terms of endemic (especially flowering) plants but it is a threatened and declining treasure.

Three thousand endemic species have been recorded in the various regions of the country. Some of them are localised in specific mountain ranges, as in the Mediterranean areas: 631 Mediterranean species are unique to the station where they can be observed. Others are more widespread, which is mostly the case in the eastern part of the country. The locality richest in terms of local endemic species is the Amanos Mountains. The regions which are the richest from the point of view of endemism are the Mugla-Antalya region, the Taurus mountains, the area around the Salt Lake, the area around Cankiri and Sivas, particularly the parts composed of native gypsum, and the northern and eastern Anatolian regions.

37

Figure 5. **WETLANDS OF INTERNATIONAL SIGNIFICANCE**

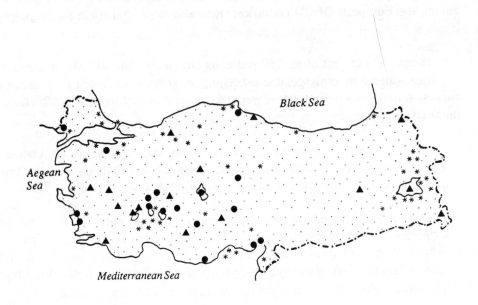

Legend:

  ● First class wetlands (16 sites; total area > 350 000 ha)
  ▲ Second class wetlands (16 sites; total area > 150 000 ha)
  * no class defined at the international level (50 sites; total area > 820 000 ha)

Sources : Ministry of Environment of the Republic of Turkey, *Turkish Background Report on Selected Environmental Topics* (1992) and Environmental Foundation of Turkey, *Wetlands of Turkey* (1989)

The intensification of the pressures arising from population growth and economic development (clearing of land for agriculture, overgrazing, forest fires, construction of dams, etc.) poses a threat to endemic plant species.

Clearing ground for fields, overgrazing, forest fires, construction of dams and the intensive frequentation of certain places are all threats for the endemic plant species.

According to a classification prepared in 1986 based on international standards, four species of endemic plants specific to Turkey have disappeared and been lost during the twentieth century. Two of these were collected from places now covered by the Keban Dam reservoir; they are assumed to have been submerged under the waters. Thirty-three other endemic species are also threatened by extinction. The distribution of 168 other endemic species is extremely limited.

Fauna - current trends

Natural ecosystems provide a habitat for many wild animal species, but encroaching development is threatening the survival of several of them.

Thanks to its geographical position and climatic and topographical characteristics, Turkey is endowed with habitats suitable for a wide variety of game and wild animal species. Its varied ecological characteristics and diverse ecosystems have made Turkey home to a wide variety of species and subspecies peculiar to the region and therefore defined as endemic. The world's largest migration of predatory birds also takes place in Turkey.

The use of agricultural pesticides and artificial fertilizers, together with intensive pollution related to industrialisation and urbanisation (toxic wastes, toxic gas, detergents and other chemicals, etc.) have had a major impact on Turkey's fauna, and several species have already become extinct.

Forest fires, both those intentionally set in order to clear forest land and those arising accidentally, are causing the destruction of the habitats of many vertebrates, including birds and mammals. Drainage of marshes, swamps and lakes eliminates aquatic fauna, including birds. In southern Turkey, for example, a bird known as the "yilanboyun" was made extinct by the draining of Lake Amik.

Introduction of exotic breeds and wild species is also a threat to the endemic fauna and flora. For example, certain species, such as the crayfish and other fish introduced into the lakes, dam reservoirs and rivers in order to increase production, disrupt the balance of those habitats, causing some local species, e.g. sheat-fish and carp, to disappear. The rainbow trout, artificially bred in Lake Abant and the nearby streams, poses a threat to the Abant trout, an endemic species. Furthermore, the viral and bacterial diseased carried by these hybrid strains constitute a hazard to the other species already living in these environments.

Game animals and some other wild animals have also declined under the pressure of hunting. Examples show the negative effects of the trade in animals, such as turtles, snails and meadow frogs, snakes and salamanders. In the seas, fishermen employ illegal equipment and flout regional and seasonal fishing prohibitions. In fresh water, dynamite, lime and high pressure liquefied gas cause mass deaths of fish.

National parks - current trends

Turkey already possesses the statutory framework for the protection of nature. Many more areas need to be placed under this protective umbrella in the next decade.

The concept of "national park" was extended in 1983 by a National Parks Law which defines several types of protected areas:

-- National park: area of great scientific or aesthetic value with recreational and touristic objectives. There is some national or international uniqueness in its natural and cultural resources. Up to 1990, 21 national parks had been created in Turkey (Figure 6).

-- Nature park: Exceptional vegetation, wild life or physio-geographical structure, contribute to the quality of the landscape. Recreational activities are allowed. In 1988, three nature parks had been designated.

-- Natural monument: site of high scientific value or containing natural phenomena which deserve specific protection.

-- Nature reserve: area devoted to scientific research and education. Should contain outstanding examples of rare, endangered or

Figure 6. PROTECTED AREAS IN TURKEY

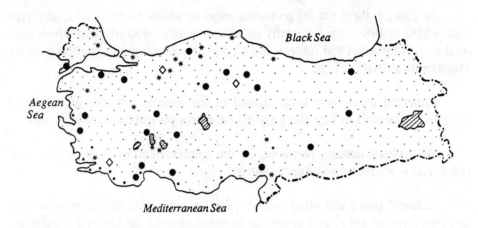

Legend :

- ● National Park
- ✳ Protection Area
- ◇ Nature Park
- · Specially Protected Area

Sources : Ministry of Environment of the Republic of Turkey, *Turkish Background Report on Selected Environmental Topics* (1992) and Environmental Foundation of Turkey, *1991 Environmental Profile of Turkey* (1991).

disappearing species, ecosystems or natural phenomena of scientific or educational importance.

--   Protection area: 18 protection areas were created in 1987 and 1988.

In Turkey, there are 90 protected areas to which 12 areas of a new type were added in 1988: the "specially protected areas". Most of them are situated on the Mediterranean and Aegean coasts, and are considered in relation with the Mediterranean Action Plan.

Protected areas have been created in the past decade, but more natural reserves are needed to face the growing pressures on habitats and ecosystems.

Difficulties remain, however, in the implementation of protection and conservation measures in protected areas.

National parks and other reserve-type areas devoted to nature protection and conservation are placed under the responsibility of the General Directorate of Forestry of the Ministry of Forestry. This causes more value to be placed on forested areas compared to other areas in terms of conservation procedures and measures. Wetlands, steppes, rocky and sandy areas, are clearly under-protected; furthermore, when dunes or wetlands are included in a protected area, the management programmes aim at developing afforestation actions, which ultimately lead to the disappearance of the original ecosystem.

Chapter 2

MANAGEMENT OF WATER RESOURCES

The development and management of Turkey's inland water resources both need to be examined in the context of the country's overall development: rapid population and industrial growth, an increasing demand for food production, and urban explosion. These factors, together with the concomitant need for health protection and conservation requirements, determine Turkey's short-term economic and environmental policy objectives. It is essential that the current policy framework be modified to embrace a more long-term view of sustainable development.

Water resource management and environmental management are closely linked and, in principle, need to be conducted through an integrated policy approach. Experiences in OECD Member countries suggest that the objective of sustainable development can only be achieved through the integrated management of water resources.

I. WATER RESOURCES

1. *Water availability and uses*

Certain regions of Turkey have a continental climate with rain throughout the year; others are characterised by a sub-tropical climate with a dry summer. Average annual rainfall is about 642 mm, with variations between 250 and 3000 mm. Consequently, Turkey is on the average well-endowed with water resources.

The time and space distribution of the country's water resource potential, however, will require substantial investment to provide for the needs of all areas.

43

Of the 501 billion m³ provided by rainfall, 186 billion m³ is estimated to reach surface waters; total renewable water resources including groundwater and inflow into the country are about 234 billion m³. (Figure 7)

Official estimates put the full development of these resources at 110 billion m³ of utilisable water -- or 47 per cent of the annual average of total water resources. Groundwater constitutes a relatively small component of total available resources (11 per cent) but it represents 17 per cent of total water withdrawal. In 1990, water requirements were estimated to be about 43 billion m³ and were expected to rise to roughly 58 billion m³ by the year 2000. Withdrawal in 1990 was 540 m³ per capita and was distributed between the major users as follows: public water supply 16.8 per cent; irrigation 71.2 per cent; industry and cooling 12 per cent. Compared to most other OECD countries the percentage use by irrigation is high. (Table 3)

The adequacy of water supply varies greatly between served and unserved populations, and within served populations. (Table 4)

For the year 2000, total withdrawals are estimated to rise by 139 per cent and consumption by 78 per cent (to 46.5 billion m³ in 2000 from 19.4 in 1985); these are considered exceptionally high increases by standards for OECD Member countries, where the average annual growth is about 1.1 per cent; however, the average per capita consumption will still be below the OECD average. The investment requirements in terms of storage dams, treatment facilities and distribution systems are clearly quite significant. These requirements could probably be reduced by an effective pricing policy combined with the upgrading of the existing technologies, particularly those used in agriculture.

A large part of the projected increase in water use is to come from the **Southeastern Anatolia Project (GAP)**. This project aims to develop the basins of the Euphrates and Tigris rivers, which together carry almost 30 per cent (52.7 billion m³) of Turkey's 186 billion m³ in total water flows. The main uses in the GAP region will be irrigation, hydro-electricity and urban consumption. At full development, irrigated land area in Turkey will be increased by about 40 per cent, an addition of 1.6 million hectares to the current 3.9 million hectares. At present, hydro-electric power supplies 6733 MW or 42 per cent of Turkey's electricity; the GAP plans to more than double present capacity with the addition of 7561 MW. Urban and industrial water uses in the region are also expected to increase rapidly, with industrial output projected to attain five times its current volume by the year 2005, and urban population to increase by 150 per cent within the same period.

Figure 7. **WATER RESOURCES**

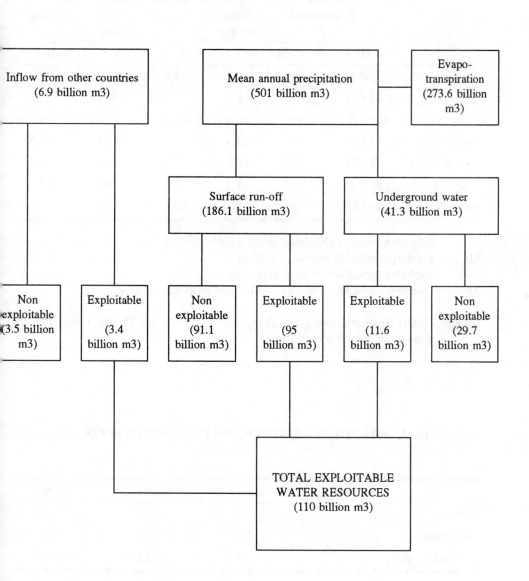

ource: Central Directorate of State Hydraulic Works, Turkey

Table 3. **TOTAL WATER WITHDRAWAL BY MAJOR USES, late 1980s**

	Water Withdrawal		Public Water Supply	Irrigation	Industry (no cooling)	Electrical Cooling
	10^6 m³	m³/cap	%	%	%	%
Turkey (a,b)	30 600	540	16.8	71.2	12.0	
Canada	43 888	1 672	11.3	7.1	9.1	55.6
USA (b)	467 000	1 952	10.8	40.5	7.4	38.8
France (b)	43 673	782	13.5	5.8	10.3	51.4
Germany (c)	44 582	728	11.0	0.5	4.9	67.4
Italy (c)	56 200	980	14.2	57.3	14.2	12.5
Spain (c,d)	45 845	1 186	11.6	65.5	22.9	

a)   Irrigation = total agricultural water withdrawal.
b)   Industry: includes industrial cooling.
c)   Excludes agriculture, except irrigation.
d)   Industry: includes industrial cooling and electrical cooling.

Source: OECD Environmental Data, Compendium (1991), and Central Directorate of State Hydraulic Works, Turkey.

Table 4. **ADEQUACY OF PUBLIC WATER SUPPLY, in 1990 (%)**

	Urban	Rural	Total
Adequate	78	60	70
Inadequate	20	25	23
No public supply	2	15	7

Source: Central Directorate of State Hydraulic Works, Turkey.

Turkey has 26 main catchment areas, with the nine **major river basins** covering 50 per cent of its entire land area. The Euphrates Basin, which covers more than 16 per cent of the country's land area and accounts for about 32 billion m³ average annual output, is the largest. The second largest river basin in terms of annual average output is the Tigris, with 21 billion m³. Both of these rivers flow into neighbouring countries (the Euphrates into Syria and the Tigris into Iraq). Their flows are subject to technical arrangements between the countries involved. Of the other seven rivers, only the Meriç, which originates in Bulgaria and forms the Turkish-Greek border, is an international river basin. Two major lakes, the Van and Salt (Tuz), receive the flows of minor river basins located in relatively dry areas. The flows of all other rivers are directed towards the surrounding seas (the Black, the Marmara, the Aegean and the Mediterranean) and, therefore, they all contribute to their pollution. The Black Sea and the Sea of Marmara, for example, are already severely polluted. (Figure 8)

Figure 8. **CATCHMENT AREAS**

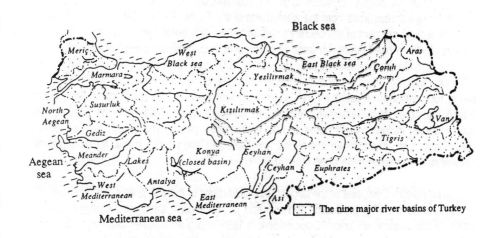

47

THE ATATURK DAM: AFFORESTATION AND EROSION CONTROL

THE EUPHRATES AND TIGRIS RIVERS IN TURKEY

	Lenght km²	Watershed km²	Flow at border billion m³/year
Euphrates	1 000	127 304	31.5
Tigris	400	57 614	21.2

The Atatürk Dam and the Southeastern Anatolia Project

The Southeastern Anatolian Project (GAP), which comprises 9.5 per cent of the national territory (a surface roughly equivalent to the area covered by the Netherlands and Belgium), aims to develop water resources from the watersheds of the Euphrates and Tigris rivers. These two rivers collect 30 per cent of the country's run-off before they enter Syria and Iraq. These water resources will be used mainly for large irrigation schemes, energy production and urban uses. Numerous hydraulic facilities are projected for the GAP area. Seven main irrigation and energy projects, including 14 dams and 11 hydro-electric plants, are located in the lower Euphrates basin; four dams are located on the Euphrates River itself: Karamis (on the Syrian border), Birecik (near the city of Gaziantep), Atatürk and Kárakaya. In the Tigris Basin there are six other main projects, including eight dams and six hydroelectric plants. The construction of some of these dams has already been completed (the Karakaya and Atatürk dams, for example) and several reservoir lakes have been created.

The Atatürk Dam, one of the largest rock-filled dams in the world, was completed in 1990 and is devoted to energy production and irrigation. Its power plant, the biggest energy-generating facility in the country, will become operational in 1992. It has an installed capacity of 2.4 billion kWh and a potential annual energy output of 8.9 billion kWh. Behind the 176 m high dam, a 817 km² lake corresponds to a total storage capacity of 48.5 billion m³. At Şanlì Urfa, a 26-km-long double tunnel will pour water from the Atatürk Dam lake into the Harran plain at the rate of 328 m³/s.

Afforestation to protect upstream slopes from erosion

Entering the Atatürk Reservoir lake, an annual flow of 26.7 billion m³ of water is expected to gradually fill up the reservoir. The evolution of land use schemes for the upstream slopes of the watershed could imply an increase of the solid load. In fact, most of the heights dominating the Atatürk Lake and the Mardin and Diyarbakir plains are uncultivated and covered with heath, or used as summer pastures. As in the entire GAP area there is almost no forest. The experience of afforestation in the Atatürk Dam area is limited. It indicates, however, that afforestation in other areas of the GAP need to be carried out with care; it should be site-specific and will have to fulfill a number of objectives, including the requirements of the local and pastoral communities. Most of the slopes drained by the run-off collected in the reservoir are unprotected; their deterioration will cause soil erosion and produce increasing loads of transported sediments if no continuous vegetation cover is planted.

To prevent the consecutive loss of volume in the reservoir, the pace of sediment delivery needs to be slowed by fighting erosion of the soils in the watersheds. Preventive actions include afforestation programmes and the promotion of soil conservation measures (i.e., terracing, buffer strip and adapted farming practices). Such action will reduce the erosion of the slopes, riverbeds and banks, and stabilize the side slopes and the siltation in the reservoirs. The 9 000 km²-area surrounding the Atatürk Dam lake will be planted with trees as part of a broader and massive tree-planting effort. This initiative targets a total afforested area of 26 350 km², or one-third of the entire GAP area. This afforestation programme has already begun, slowly, in certain areas.

Integrated watershed management

Further conservation problems may arise in relation to tree-planting efforts. The planned forests will extend over barren mountainous areas as well as over land presently used as extensive pasture for herds of sheep and cattle. It is expected that the pasture land will suffer and decrease from these afforestation and irrigation programmes; summits will be planted and foothills cultivated for farming. Therefore, conflicts between forestry services, shepherds, and farmers should be forestalled in the early stages of the programme.

At a later stage, to prevent their deterioration, pasture and forest areas should be carefully protected from over-cutting for fuelwood and wood production, over-cultivation and excessive livestock grazing. This will require an integrated management of the watersheds through a co-ordination of forestry, farming, and cattle-raising practices.

2. Water quality

By 1989, water quality monitoring undertaken by the State Hydraulic Works (SHW) was extended to cover 679 sampling stations. The **major sources of pollution** are:

-- **Domestic waste water**: Rural settlements (41 per cent of the population by the year 1990) are not served by a public sewer system. Urban settlements have the following characteristics: 56 per cent have sewerage collection systems of which only 6 per cent have wastewater treatment; 43 per cent are served with septic tanks (see also under Chapter 3 - Water Pollution).

-- **Industrial waste water**: In the process of producing 26.9 per cent of GNP, industry discharges its waste water into rivers or other water areas. Ninety-eight percent of the Turkish industries do not have wastewater treatment facilities and those that do are either inefficient or not operating properly.

-- **Agricultural pollution** consists mainly of: fertilizer run-off (5.9 million tonnes of fertilizer were used in 1990, according to the definition used by the Turkish authorities); insecticide use (34.6 thousands tonnes in 1989); and run-off from animal husbandry (33 per cent of total agricultural output).

Rough estimates put total organic wastewater load (excluding agricultural pollution) at around 85 million population equivalent (PE), of which 60 million PE comes from communities and 20-25 million PE from industry. Total BOD load into surface water is estimated between 3000 to 5000 tonnes daily - or an average input into surface waters of 10-15 mg per liter. Untreated industrial wastewater contributes various toxic compounds. Quality parameters and calculations for the individual annual loads and physico-chemical characteristics of most of the major rivers are available from the State Hydraulic Works. Both types of indicators suggest serious river pollution and consequent coastal water pollution.

Discharges from a variety of sources are almost certainly affecting **groundwater** resources. Although only anecdotal evidence is available on groundwater quality, it is clear that discharges from a large number of septic tanks and latrines as well as from industrial sources and agricultural activities are leached into groundwater sources. In some areas urban wastewater is discharged into underground caverns where it can also penetrate into groundwater supply sources, particularly in the Antalya region and in Küçükçekmece Springs in the Istanbul region.

Sufficient information was not available to assess the quality of Turkey's surface waters (rivers and lakes). The general lack of wastewater treatment facilities, however, suggests there must be significant water quality problems, at least at a localised level. The projected increases in future water demand and industrial activity cannot fail to heighten the threat to the nation's natural waters, unless new steps are taken to better integrate water resource management.

II. INSTITUTIONAL AND LEGAL FRAMEWORK

1. *Institutional arrangements*

The responsibility for the development, management, protection and conservation of water resources is shouldered by numerous ministries and agencies, but the main responsible authority is the Ministry of Public Works and Settlement.

The **Ministry of Public Works and Settlement** has two main agencies responsible for the major components of water resource development and management: **the State Hydraulic Works** and **the Bank of Provinces**. Their main responsibilities are: development of water resources (e.g., dam construction), and management of water resources such as drainage, irrigation, flood mitigation, water supply treatment, and wastewater disposal. Under these agencies, in metropolitan areas, provision of water and sewerage systems are the responsibility of Metropolitan Authorities. In reality, the State Hydraulic Works, with its various responsibilities for planning, monitoring and implementation, bears primary responsibility for the sustainable development of water resources. The Bank of Provinces also has a strong influence on waste water disposal and water quality through its financing activities.

The **Ministry of Agriculture and Urban Affairs,** together with the Ministry of Public Works, is responsible for irrigation, aquaculture, water supply, and related projects in the rural areas.

The **Ministry of Health,** through its general health services branch, is the main agency for the hygiene control of drinking water. It is empowered to set water quality standards and monitor their implementation.

The **State Planning Organisation** (SPO) prepares submissions to the government for the annual and quinquennial investment programmes for water resource development and waste water treatment plants; the objective is to present rational, coherent and consistent investment programmes. In principle, the SPO establishes investment priorities, taking economic, social and environmental factors into consideration.

The **Ministry of Environment** (previously attached to the Prime Ministry as Undersecretariat to the Ministry of State) was only recently elevated to ministry status and designated as the main co-ordinating body for environmental management. As a ministry, it is therefore charged with co-ordinating all national and international activities concerning water resources. Its organisational structure provides for Province Environment Directorates authorised to decide on water related issues. These provincial directorates, however, have yet to be established. (Figure 9)

In **the Metropolitan Municipalities** (eight out of 73 province capital municipalities), the Metropolitan Authority (a combination of the district municipalities) is responsible for implementing pollution control policies, including the construction and operation of sewage treatment facilities.

2. *Legal aspects, regulations and standards*

As defined by the constitution, control over all ground and common surface waters, with the exception of some privately owned springs and small waters, is vested in the government.

Under the **Environment Law of 1983,** the "Regulation of Water Pollution Control" was promulgated in 1988. According to this regulation, all inland waters are classified into four quality classes, each of which have specific standards for water quality parameters. Industrial effluent discharge criteria are also stated in the regulation. The State Hydraulic Works is responsible for the classification of surface inland waters (under a different law, promulgated in 1961, the agency also has the implied responsibility for groundwater).

The **General Public Health Law** sets down public health and pollution control requirements, but these requirements are insufficient to prevent the pollution of water resources. There are specific regulations on waste water in the Metropolitan Areas.

Figure 9. INSTITUTIONAL FRAMEWORK OF WATER RESOURCE MANAGEMENT

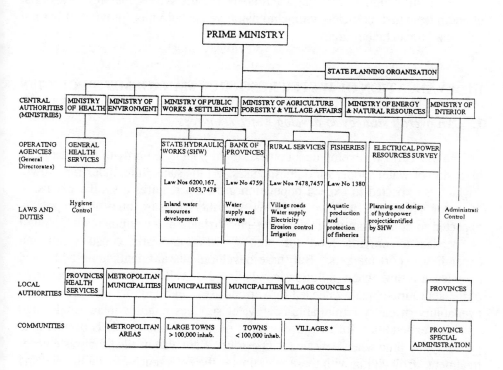

* Villages without any municipal organisation

Source : Ministry of Environment of the Republic of Turkey. *Turkish Background Report on Selected Environmental Topics* (1992).

The Environment Law is intended to provide a sufficient legal basis for Environmental Impact Assessment (EIA), which can be used to recommend ways to prevent water polluting activities.

For administrative purposes, the State Hydraulic Works operates 25 regional directorates which coincide with administrative spatial units (provinces) but not with the 26 catchment areas.

III. EVALUATION OF WATER RESOURCE MANAGEMENT POLICIES

1. *An overall strategy to develop water resources*

In the Turkish development context, rapid population growth requires rapid extension of water supply for domestic uses. At the same time, industrial growth - which is expected to exceed population growth - requires a similar extension of water supply for its own purposes. Further pressure on water supply is expected to come from the major, projected irrigation developments which will be needed to provide food for both growing domestic consumption and expanding export markets. But these developments are demanding additional supplies at a time when pollution is reducing the availability of water resources of the appropriate quality needed for various uses. Furthermore, the diminishing availability of easily exploitable new water supplies requires increasingly high levels of expenditure for the development of new supplies; this is occurring at precisely the time when new financial resources are also needed for waste water treatment. Coinciding with these pressures is the emergence of a public demand for environmental quality, particularly in the field of water services. This demand, which is increasingly vocal, though still only locally based, is in accordance with Turkey's international aspirations in the field of water resources. It is, therefore, both **an economic and an environmental necessity that water resources be developed in a sustainable manner**.

Integrated management is now generally recognised to be the only way to achieve sustainable development. This will require a change in the approach still prevailing in the organisations responsible for water resource development in Turkey. For instance, the figures on projected water withdrawals, taken from the Turkish Background Report, are an example of the supply management approach typical of large engineering organisations. (Table 5)

In order to move towards integrated management, certain elements in water resource management have to be recognised and managed in a co-ordinated manner; these include integration between:

54

Table 5. OUTLOOK FOR WATER REQUIREMENTS AND WITHDRAWAL

	WATER REQUIREMENTS (a)		WATER WITHDRAWAL (b)		
	Billion m³	% of fully exploitable resources (c)	Billion m³	% of fully exploitable resources (c)	% of total water resources (d)
1985	36.0	33	19.4	18	8.3
1990	43.3	39	30.6	28	13.1
1995	50.6	46	40.2	37	17.2
2000	58.1	53	46.5	42	20.0

a) Water requirements as estimated in 1985 by the State Hydraulic Works for major users of the water resources. (Due to budgetary constraints on retaining the rights to full exploitation and distribution of water resources, these requirements do not match the water withdrawal.) Requirements do not take into account successive uses of the same water volume.

b) Estimated water withdrawal to be supplied to major users of water resources.

c) Technically and economically exploitable water resources amount to 106.6 billion m³, plus an additional 3.4 billion m³ exploitable inflow from neighbouring countries.

d) Total water resources include exploitable and non-exploitable surface and underground waters, plus inflow from neighbouring countries.

Source: Central Directorate for State Hydraulic Works, Turkey.

-- Present and future uses (the long-term horizon);

-- All uses within a river basin (river basin management);

-- Surface and ground water uses;

-- Inland and coastal waters;

-- Related natural resources (water, land, forest);

-- Quantity and quality management;

-- National and international waters.

Integrating these elements effectively at minimal administrative cost and maximal economic and environmental efficiency requires a certain institutional framework: administration and water rights legislation; and a set of policies, including demand and supply management; and a water quality strategy.

2. *Elements of integration*

This assessment of the broad principles and practices governing water resource management in Turkey suggests that certain **elements of integration** have been incorporated into policy formulation and integration. However, the emphasis in Turkey has been on securing supplies, with less importance attached to economic efficiency and to environmental concerns:

-- Although plans exist for better integration to ensure adequate and economically justifiable supplies for future generations, they have yet to be put into effect;

-- The co-ordination of ground and surface water resource uses to ensure that high quality groundwater is supplied only for high quality uses, has yet to be implemented;

-- Inland and coastal waters are not managed in a mutually beneficial manner, despite full recognition of the need for greater co-ordination; at present, inland waters are the major source of coastal pollution; consequently, coastal water management is seriously jeopardised;

-- The need for the integration of water and other natural resources (land and forest), although recognised in principle, is only practised in certain regions as part of forestry policy;

-- In water use and disposal policies there appears to be only limited recognition of the potential benefit of economically efficient water use on water quality; similarly, awareness of the negative impact of pollution on water supply is weak. This lack of integration is one of the weakest elements in Turkey's water resource policy.

The need for co-operation with neighbouring countries is well recognised and accepted. Technical arrangements for sharing common resources do exist. Considerable progress has been made in cleaning up communally polluted waters, such as the Black Sea. A convention concerning the protection and cleaning up of the Black Sea was signed in April 1992; the activity centre will be Istanbul.

3. *Institutional framework*

The **institutional framework** for integrated management in Turkey at the central governmental level exists, but it is basically oriented towards providing additional water supplies. Quality management, which is also included under the responsibility of the Ministry of Public Works and Settlement, has not been fully implemented or co-ordinated with other responsible authorities. Co-ordination for irrigation requirements between the Ministry of Agriculture and Rural Affairs and the Ministry of Public Works and Settlement is close, but does not include sufficient consideration of environmental consequences.

Reconciliation of **the competing policy objectives** of economic growth, environmental quality and conservation, to the extent that this is regarded as an issue, is undertaken largely by the State Planning Organisation. This is carried out through the allocation of investment priorities for infrastructure on water supply and sewerage facilities. No attempts have been made to assess potential conflicts or to reconcile these policies from the environmental point of view. For example, the potential environmental consequences of large-scale irrigation under the GAP have not been evaluated properly and hence are not integrated in the investment process. Some projects on EIA in the GAP region have now been started. Also missing from the investment process is a proper economic evaluation of the GAP, including an assessment of its long-term environmental costs and benefits.

Co-operation between central and local authorities consists mainly in the implementation of centrally designed policies at the local level. At present, the Governor, as the representative of the central government, has the co-ordinating role with considerable discretionary powers. This situation has resulted in two apparent consequences:

-- Local authorities, apart from the eight Metropolitan Areas, play a minor role in water resource management and cannot enforce their environmental priorities;

-- Considerable differences can occur from one region to another in the provision of water and sewerage services.

Public consultation, as part of the integration process, appears to be lacking in water resource management. Furthermore, channels for public input or influence on the policies of the authorities appear to be limited and rarely accessed.

4. *Supply and demand management*

Supply and demand management is based at present on water requirements. These requirements are in turn projected on the basis of sectoral growth forecasts by the State Hydraulic Works, rather than on demand forecasts using alternative price assumptions. This method of forecasting water requirements fails to take into account: the possibility of changing technologies in water use; the potential improvements in water use efficiency through appropriate pricing; and the environmental consequences of a supply policy aimed at satisfying "requirements".

This approach results in a **supply-driven policy** rather than comprehensive supply management. More specifically, the process of decision-making that currently exists for investment in the development of individual sources of supply is unclear. It is questionable whether proper cost/benefit analysis is employed and, if so, to what extent it assesses the environmental costs of supply development, such as changes in landscape, sedimentation, etc. Decisions on investments appear to be reached solely by the State Hydraulic Works and then only on purely technical grounds; if consultation does take place between the various authorities (environmental and local), it is neither a systematic nor an institutionalised process for integrated decision-making.

Only scant information pertaining to the cost of the supply system appears to exist or to be easily accessible. Moreover, given the current scarcity of data, it is impossible to compare expenditure data for investment or operation of the supply system on a nation-wide or even on a regional basis. Data on individual projects, such as the GAP, are available, but not on a comparative basis. This lack of information raises questions about the economic aspects of management.

Demand management of water services should consist of a number of specific elements: demand forecasting, water rights allocation, water services pricing, and regulatory mechanisms for managing demand. The question of demand forecasting leads to the conclusion that such forecasting needs to be considerably strengthened if supply management is to be more effective.

All **water rights**, with minor exceptions, are vested in the state. This principle, however, allows private abstraction from groundwater and surface waters through adjoining owners. The division of ownership and related responsibilities between central and local authorities lacks clear definition.

Pricing of water services is underdeveloped in Turkey. Recent data suggest that recoveries of capital costs in the irrigation sector (excluding interest charges, which are carried by the state) amounted to 51 per cent and 74 per cent of operation and maintenance costs respectively. The government has proposed that capital costs include interest, with a reduced repayment period and adjustment for inflation, 100 per cent recovery of operation and maintenance, and increased penalties for non-payment. No information is available on pricing methods used for hydro-electricity, but there are indications that water is provided at well below real cost. Public water supply revenues only cover current operating expenses.

In none of these sectors are **environmental costs included in the price** of water services. Indeed, no attempt appears to have been made to even assess the magnitude of environmental impacts, despite the fact that a review of parts of the GAP project suggests that they could be significant. As a result, water pricing in Turkey, from both the economic and the environmental point of view, is seriously deficient.

Regulatory mechanisms for demand management consist largely of restrictions on water use during shortages. One way of regulating demand is to withhold supply connections from areas where illegal constructions are located. Regulations concerning the installation of water-using appliances, whether for household, industrial, or irrigation system use, appear to be infrequently applied. On the whole, and excepting the withholding of water supply to illegal

59

construction areas, the use of regulatory mechanisms for demand management is very limited and could be substantially extended.

Sectoral management of demand for water services is currently weak. With the exception of the measures described above, there is neither a consistent strategy for water-using sectors, nor any overall, sectorally-targeted strategy to optimise water use in geographic areas with heavy polluting activities (for example, those where leather and food-processing industries, and irrigation on certain types of soil, are concentrated).

5. *Water quality management*

The accepted approach to water quality management in OECD countries is composed of the following elements: goal setting, problem assessment by source, standards for permits, compliance, enforcement, public financing, pollution prevention, specific areas, such as wetlands, and groundwater. Certain elements of this strategy have been developed in Turkey, but the serious and continuing deterioration of both surface and groundwater quality suggest a need for the reinforcement of the existing strategy.

Goal setting for quality of water resources is at present health-oriented in order to minimise the potential impacts of bacteria and chemicals contained in water. These health criteria might be regarded as a minimum compared with the economic and ecological criteria which other countries have begun to use. Even the health risk criteria in Turkey are narrowly defined and concentrate mainly on bacteriological risks.

Problem assessment by source has been carried out for point sources of pollution both for municipal wastewater and for industrial wastewater. Data are based both on monitoring and on calculated inputs from manufacturing activities. There is no crosschecking of this information to establish its reliability. There is also a lack of longer-term time trend data needed to measure progress in water quality management.

Standards and permit systems for municipal and major point sources in Turkey vary substantially from case to case. As only a few sewage treatment plants exist, no discharge standards are currently set for municipal wastewater. For some of the most polluted areas, such as the Izmit Bay, a "Best Practicable Treatment" (BPT) standard is set for certain industries. However, the majority of industries fail to adhere to this practice and have no treatment facilities at all. Not a single case of the imposition of the "Best Available Economically

Achievable Treatment" (BAT) standard has been reported. Nor have there been any reports of instances where permits prescribed an effluent discharge limit based on water quality standards (also referred to as "Water Quality Based Limits").

One innovative approach used in Turkey is the "industrial park" or "Organised Industrial Estate" establishment, where medium- and small-sized industries share basic treatment facilities so as to benefit from economies of scale in investment and operating costs. The efficacy of this approach, which is fairly recent, will depend on both the effectiveness of treatment and the degree of enforcement.

Non-point sources of pollution have, to date, gone largely uncontrolled in Turkey, with the exception of a few, very specific areas believed to be of high environmental value. Situations of severe water pollution by pesticides have already been identified and require the immediate application of control measures.

Compliance is based, by and large, on self-monitoring and reporting by the permittee establishment. It is not known how wide-spread the system is, nor how often reporting is required. The effectiveness of this system, which is not open to public scrutiny and is poorly monitored by public authorities, is unclear.

Enforcement is generally weak, given the lack of information and the vaguely defined nature of the standards. Fines, when imposed, are low and economic instruments in the form of effluent charges are not used. Subsidies for pollution control, although not on a large scale, are given to assist industry. On the whole, present enforcement policy fails to lead to technological innovation in pollution control. Considerable tightening will be needed to halt the rising trend in wastewater discharge.

Public financing is the accepted method of financing municipal wastewater collection and treatment. A substantial portion of these funds, which are provided by the central government, are allocated on a grant basis. These funds, however, are insufficient to provide facilities for the existing population, let alone for future population growth. This method of financing also falls short of full compliance with the Polluter-Pays-Principle. With the exception of the eight Metropolitan areas, the ability of local governments to raise money for financing wastewater infrastructure is weak. Political will to impose appropriate charges also appears to be lacking.

Pollution prevention policies aimed at moving from an end-of-pipe treatment approach to one based on source reduction, water conservation and water reclamation, are to be developed and should include specific environmental impact assessment procedures.

Wetlands protection can be regarded as a combined problem of water quantity and quality management. Wetlands, in addition to being habitats of major ecological importance, are now recognised as crucial to the hydrological cycle. Turkey intends to become a party soon to the Ramsar Convention and has taken steps to protect certain major wetlands with large bird populations. However, many of Turkey's roughly one million so-called "wetlands" are unprotected and are currently being polluted and/or drained.

Groundwater, as mentioned earlier, is the major source of drinking water supply and as such needs to be fully protected and allocated only for high quality uses. Although legislation on "Underground Waters" exists, their protection appears to be neglected, at least in certain areas. With the spread of irrigation practices, the pollution threat to groundwater is also increasing. To date, little, if any, effort has been made to protect groundwater from the increasing variety of potential pollution sources, such as agricultural chemicals, septic tanks and waste dumps.

IV. RECOMMENDATIONS FOR IMPROVED WATER RESOURCE MANAGEMENT

Overall economic development in Turkey relies on the capacity of inland water resources management to: supply drinking water and sanitation facilities to the country's rapidly increasing urban and rural populations; provide water inputs for agricultural production; and contribute positively to the country's trade balance. Water inputs are also of crucial importance to industry and to the production of hydro-electricity. Fresh water resources are of major environmental and biological importance and are the basic life support systems, not only for man but also for all of nature's ecosystems.

Sustainable development of the inland water resource of Turkey is therefore **an essential economic and environmental goal** to be achieved through wise and efficient management.

Turkey has a strong tradition of state planning in water resource management. The current approach is project-oriented and driven by perceived demand requirements. Major development projects, which have either been completed or are under construction, will serve multi-purpose development objectives, notably, the GAP programme. These projects not only attest to the engineering, administrative, and institutional capabilities of the country, they also respond to urgent water supply needs.

1. *Adoption of an integrated water resource management strategy*

Integrated water resource management based on the existing administrative framework should be the fundamental approach to achieve economic efficiency and the improvement of the environment. However, improvements are urgently needed to achieve integrated management. Further deterioration of water quality together with the misuse and overuse of water resources could create a serious public health hazard, lead to severe damage to water resources, and undermine Turkey's overall development. Specifically, an acceleration of investment in wastewater treatment is needed to counteract the deterioration of inland and coastal water quality. Increased investment in wastewater treatment would also improve health, while generating tourism and other economic benefits. Water development projects, for instance, should be evaluated economically through the traditional cost/benefit analysis method, and environmentally on the basis of environmental impact assessments (EIAs). These two methods could be combined in cases where sufficient data are generated.

Closer links should first be established between authorities - and hence policies - dealing with the following water services:

-- Water supply (domestic, industrial, agricultural);

-- Pollution control and water treatment, involving the establishment, monitoring and enforcement of standards;

-- Flood control;

-- Navigation;

-- Hydro-electricity production; and

-- Amenities.

These authorities should adopt **guiding principles** for water resource management of the type now broadly accepted in OECD Member countries:

-- The allocation of water supply investment according to demand for services based on proper pricing policies;

-- The integration of water quantity and quality management in a mutually supportive manner;

-- The joint management of surface and groundwater, and the recognition of the high value of groundwater;

-- The recognition of the close relationship between inland and coastal water in any management of inland waters;

-- The reconciliation of water, land and forestry policies in light of their mutual impacts.

To put these guiding principles into practice, a **number of actions** should be taken at central government level to create the necessary conditions for integrated water resource management:

-- An appropriate administrative framework for integrated management of water resources;

-- The necessary legal arrangements for policy implementation;

-- The measures needed to implement policies, including funding mechanisms.

2. *Administrative framework*

While the present OECD review of the environmental policies in Turkey is a partial one focusing on just three policy areas, some of the conclusions are applicable in a wider sense. Moreover, the **integration of policy objectives** has emerged as an important theme of much of recent OECD work. Thus, integrated water resource management must be considered in the context of the integration of all environment/economy inter-actions.

The proposals that follow should be read in that light and therefore do not go beyond the brief of the OECD mission.

Given the Turkish government's stated commitment to sustainable development, it is vital that economic and environmental issues be considered at the highest political level, i.e. in Cabinet.

One way to bring this about would be to establish an Environment/Natural Resource Cabinet Committee in which ministers could discuss water resource and other economy/environment issues. Such a Cabinet Committee would reflect Turkey's political willingness both to integrate policy and to harmonize the country's economic development and environmental quality goals. The main areas requiring serious attention appear to be: the agricultural use of water and long-term soil productivity; water pollution caused in the course of agricultural and industrial activity and the development of tourism; inadequate wastewater treatment and the protection of public health; and, finally, economic efficiency and the waste of natural resources.

An alternative arrangement would be to make the Minister of Environment an automatic member of all economic development Cabinet Committees. The comparative merits of these two arrangements are further discussed in Chapter 5 of this report, but whatever option is preferred by the Turkish government, the Cabinet Structure should be mirrored at the public service level by a standing committee or a series of *ad hoc*, inter-departmental committees of officials. More particularly, all water resource issues could then be dealt with by an official committee consisting of representatives from departments involved in water resource policies as well as those dependent on water services.

In terms of the future role of the Ministry of Environment, there are several aspects to consider:

Local presence: The Turkish government is already moving towards a greater decentralisation of many of its functions, and environmental administration certainly also needs a greater "on-the-spot" presence of the Ministry of Environment. It is also one of the themes of this report that there is a need for a greater local involvement in water resource management, and in environmental management generally.

Range of responsiblilities: The new Ministry of Environment currently has only a policy and co-ordinating role while regulatory powers are still vested in the long-established departments. One of the main conclusions of this review is that the required strengthening of enforcement can best be achieved if the regulatory functions are moved away from departments whose main focus is not oriented towards the environment.

Taking account of all this, it is possible to formulate three options in which the above considerations have been given different "weightings".

These three options do not take account of the more recent decision of the Turkish government to establish a Provincial Environment Directorate in each of the country's 73 provinces. While this would meet the need for a greater on-the-spot presence of the Ministry of Environment, there are two potential problems with such a move. First, the scale of many environmental problems is larger than the average size of a province. This means that a considerable amount of co-ordination between groups of Provincial Environment Directorates would be required. Secondly, it may prove difficult to provide the necessary expertise on so many different issues in so many places.

The first option could be called "status quo plus" and constitutes the option of minimum change. The present responsibilities of the Ministry of Environment and the other ministries remain unchanged, but resourcing is increased to allow the various environmental functions - particularly enforcement of policies and consent procedures - to be carried out more rigorously and effectively. It is the easiest option to implement and the most feasible option in the short run, but it will not be sufficient to meet future long-term challenges.

The second option is called "integrated management plus deconcentration". It involves extending the responsibilities of the Ministry of Environment to enable it to formulate and enforce national policies and standards. Much of the work would be devolved to the Regional Directorates of the Ministry which would perhaps number around 15 covering the entire country and whose boundaries would coincide with those of major river basins. The Ministry's Head Office would remain responsible for legislation, formulating national policies and standards, and research. The Regional Directorates would draw up indicative river basin management plans, enforce regulations and standards, and carry out environmental monitoring. The Regional Directorates would also have a major role in the co-ordination between various regional offices of government departments and the municipalities, especially in the area of coastal zone management (see Chapter 4). This option would represent a greater change from the status quo, but would be better suited for integrated environment management than the first option. It would require, however, much time to be introduced.

Finally, the third option could be called "integrated management plus local decision-making". Again regulatory and enforcement powers would be transferred from the State Hydraulic Works and the Ministry of Health. The Head Office of the Ministry of Environment would have much the same role as under the previous option. The main difference compared with the second option is that most of the regional responsibilities would be given to newly created Regional Environment Agencies which would be regionally elected and funded, giving them a certain independence from central government (a fuller description of their functions is given below). The main role of the Regional Directorates of the Ministry of Environment would be to provide advice to the Governor's Office, co-ordinate the environmental responsibilities of the various central government departments and oversee the operations of the Regional Environment Agencies. Over the long term this option would provide solutions both for integrating and for decentralising environmental policies.

The State Hydraulic Works would continue to be responsible for water resource development through the building of dams, main pipelines, etc. These activities would be conducted according to the demand projections prepared by the Regional Environment Agencies and jointly agreed to by the State Planning Organisation and the State Hydraulic Works. All development work undertaken by the State Hydraulic Works should be subjected to EIAs and approved by the Ministry of Environment.

The Regional Directorates of the Ministry of Environment (Option 2) or the Regional Environment Agencies (Option 3), whose administrative boundaries would be the natural watershed, would have the following responsibilities in the field of water management:

-- Management of the watershed to ensure that all aspects of water services are fairly represented in the decision-making process (drinking water, irrigation, wastewater disposal, recreation, wetlands, wildlife, forests, recreation, cultural values);

-- Co-ordination for water planning and land use planning, including soil conservation;

-- Efficient demand management of all water services in conjunction with the local authorities: this should include implementation of water pricing policy as defined by the national authorities;

-- Overall management of the rivers under their authority for minimum flows and allocation of permits for various industrial, agricultural, and hydro-electric uses; this should include ensuring proper auditing of EIAs;

-- Integrated quantity and quality management and pollution control: the setting of standards, monitoring discharge, and the allocation and enforcement of permits;

-- Preparation of demand projections for their respective river basins with the assistance of the SHW and the municipalities;

-- Integrated management of surface and groundwater;

-- Setting of resource rentals, pollution charges and penalties in co-operation with the municipalities and the respective Governors; responsibility for the redistribution of these revenues for pollution control purposes;

-- Monitoring of water quality;

-- Giving account of their activities to the Ministry of Environment and the public at large.

The following chapters in this report will suggest additional functions of the proposed Regional Environment Agencies in the fields of coastal zone management and air quality management.

The Ministry of Health should continue to assist in the setting of standards for drinking water and bathing water. However, it would appear to be more efficient to transfer the department's monitoring responsibilities to the Ministry of Environment, i.e. to the proposed Regional Environment Agencies.

The Bank of Provinces, in co-operation with the Regional Environment Agencies, should continue to finance and construct water supply and sewerage systems for the smaller municipalities.

3. *Legal arrangements*

In terms of water resource legislation, Turkey, like other OECD Member countries, provides a general legal framework for its management and development. Turkey defines both water rights and controls over the use of water, sets out general policy objectives for administrative agencies, defines their responsibilities and, to some degree, lays down consultation procedures both between authorities and the public. These laws are designed to ensure a fair and equitable supply to all users. However, with the alteration of conditions over time, these laws have also become serious constraints on integrated and efficient management. Different acts correspond to the various different uses of water services and their end-users; for example, acts exist for water supply and transport, flood mitigation, energy generation, recreation, and for environmental protection and conservation. It is **essential that existing legislation** in these fields **be reviewed** with the following objectives:

-- ensuring consistency of all legislation dealing with water resources, particularly with regard to their ownership, environmental protection, conservation, and allocation;

-- clarifying the degree of governmental control currently retained with respect to users' rights and responsibilities. The limits to these rights should be defined in a way that respects a variety of social objectives, such as environmental protection, cultural preservation, and free market competition;

-- prescribing the use of **economic principles**, such as the User-Pays and the Polluter-Pays concepts, as well as of **economic instruments, regulatory schemes, enforcement procedures**. Under the User-Pays concept consumers or users of drinking water, industrial users, irrigation users, recreational water users, flood mitigation beneficiaries etc. should pay for the cost of provision, delivery and depletion cost of water. **Water pricing principles and practices** for the main consumers (households, industry and agriculture) should also be explicitly prescribed by legislation;

-- prescribing the basic responsibilities and co-ordination mechanism for water resource administration.

4. *Policy implementation*

Policy implementation can be improved by increasing attention to the environmental dimensions of major water development projects and through a shift in emphasis from water supply development to demand management, including a greater reliance on economic instruments. These changes would, in turn, generate more funds for environmental protection, particularly wastewater treatment.

Major development projects like the GAP should be constructed and operated in conformity with the above recommendations, with particular attention to the following objectives:

-- The mandatory EIA of all plans for the construction of dams, hydro-power plants, irrigation channels and other structures;

-- The application of appropriate erosion control measures should be taken to protect the river basin;

-- The examination of all areas designated for irrigation in terms of their capability to sustain long-term irrigation, and the identification of measures to protect soils from deterioration;

-- The provision of training in sustainable irrigation management for farmers working in irrigated areas.

Water resource management should be led by **demand management** of water services particularly with regard to consumptive uses such as in households, industry, and agriculture but should also be applied to hydro-electricity, flood mitigation and recreation:

-- **Demand forecasting** should be based on explicit price assumptions and should incorporate alternative technical, economic, environmental and financial appraisals; linear projections of past trends are not useful methods for rational supply management;

-- **Pricing of water and sewage services** should be based on the "User-Pays Principle" and should be applied to water supplies and sewage services. The price of water should cover the capital, operation, maintenance, and environmental costs of providing water; capital costs should be recovered over 25 to 30 years at the bond rate of interest. Also, price should reflect the long-term incremental costs to the community of satisfying marginal demand; such charging system is usually referred to as "the long-run marginal social cost pricing". A similar approach should be used to calculate sewage charges. These charging systems should be used both to manage demand and to raise revenues. To achieve an effective and equitable water use, the major consumers, at the very least, need to be metered and charged accordingly.

-- **Other measures** need to be used in conjunction with pricing; these include: plumbing codes, regulations on water installations, irrigation practices, and industrial uses of water. Operational controls should be used for leak detection in water supplies, and an extensive consumer information system should be set up to educate the public to the financial and environmental benefits of water conservation. A special programme of agricultural extension services should also be devised to educate farmers in cost-effective and sustainable irrigation agriculture.

Formulation and implementation of a **water quality strategy** is a major component of water resource management. Turkey has developed parts of this strategy and this framework needs to be applied in a more complete form consisting of the following elements:

-- Development of an information base for the comprehensive understanding of present and likely future water quality problems;

-- The establishment of water quality goals and standards to preserve water resource quality;

-- The identification of sources of present and future contamination;

-- The evaluation and implementation of options for solving and preventing water contamination;

-- The specification of requirements for individual sources to attain goals and meet standards; the measurement of their achievements; the issuance of permits for water discharges and their enforcement through regulations and economic instruments;

-- The identification of needs for public financial assistance, particularly in terms of grants to local authorities for the construction of wastewater treatment plants.

Because Turkey occupies a strategic position in Southeastern Europe and in the Middle East, **international co-operation** also needs to be a central element of water resource management. Such co-operation is needed for a region-wide sustainable development, including a fair distribution and long-term development of water resources. These objectives could be best achieved through economically and environmentally efficient and consistent demand and supply management. Such an approach would ensure water resources of the appropriate quality provided that all participants follow similar policies.

Chapter 3

URBAN POLLUTION

I. CONTEXT OF URBAN ENVIRONMENTAL PROBLEMS

1. *Demographic trends*

The population of Turkey reached 56 million in 1990. The annual population growth rate has declined in the past decade from 2.6 per cent in 1971-1972 to 2.3 per cent in 1988-1989 but is still high when compared with other OECD countries. (Table 6)

2. *Urbanisation and development trends*

A positive migration rate plus the high natural growth rate gives rise to a very high growth rate of urban population (4.7 per cent in 1990). Today 33 million people live in urban areas; this number is expected to reach 45 million in 2000.

Unlike other OECD countries, Turkey is experiencing a recent and very rapid urbanisation process. The ratio of urban population compared to total population, which was only 25.4 per cent in 1950 and 38 per cent in 1970, was approaching 60 per cent in 1991. (Figure 10)

The rapid growth of towns leads to the expansion of suburbs and the overcrowding of city-centres, which are not equipped to cope with this concentration: the annual growth rate of the city-centre of Bursa, for example, was 7 per cent in 1989 while the urban population of the area grew overall by 3.5 per cent. Urban growth at such a great pace creates a wide variety of environmental problems.

Table 6. POPULATION TRENDS, 1970-1990

	Total population						Urban population (a)			
	Total population (1000 inhab.)			Change (%)	Average annual growth rate (%)		Share in total population (%)		Annual growth rate (%)	
	1970	1980	1990	1970-90	1971-72	1989-90	1970	1990	1970	1990 b)
Turkey	35 605	44 737	56 471	58.6	2.6	2.3	38	57c)	3.6	4.7c)
Canada	21 297	24 042	26 603	24.9	1.1	1.2	76	76	1.2	1.0
USA	205 052	227 757	251 523	22.7	1.1	1.0	74	74	1.1	0.8
France	50 772	53 880	56 420	11.1	0.9	0.5	71	74	0.9	0.6
w. Germany	60 651	61 566	62 063 d)	2.3	0.6	0.9	81	86	0.5	0.1
Italy	52 771	55 657	56 937	7.9	0.7	0.1	64	69	0.0	0.5
Spain	33 646	37 386	38 959	15.8	0.9	0.2	66	78	0.6	0.1

a) The precise definition of an urban area varies between countries. Most countries define an urban area as a locality containing a minimum population of between 2000 to 5000.
b) Projected annual growth for 1990-1995.
c) 1990 data provided by Turkish National Statistics.
d) 1989 data provided by Turkish National Statistics.

Source: OECD population data and UN urban population data quoted from UNEP, *Environmental Data Report 1991/92* (1991).

Figure 10. **URBANISATION TRENDS, 1927-1990**

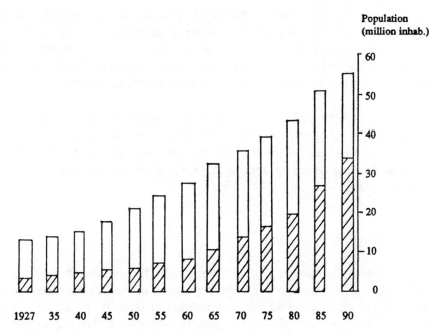

Population
(million inhab.)

Legend :
Total population
Population in towns and urban districts

Source : State Institute of Statistics. *Statistical Indicators 1923-1990* (1991)

In Turkey, physical planning is considered the most important environmental instrument. In the six successive five-year development plans (the VIth covers the period 1990-1994) specific objectives of territorial planning:

-- promote the growth of existing medium-sized cities relative to that of the metropolitan areas;

-- divert population movements from west to east, with the implementation of projects such as GAP.

Specific measures to sustain this policy include such incentives as tax reductions, favourable credit terms and better wages.

Migrations

Until the 1950s, Turkey was predominantly an agricultural country with about 80 per cent of the population living in rural areas. Modernisation of agriculture and changes in the occupation of land contributed to the destabilisation of the rural society while people in search of a job migrated from villages to cities and also to foreign countries such as Germany.

Some regions of Turkey furnish more migrants than other regions: in the eastern and southeastern parts of the country, the rural exodus has led more and more people to migrate towards the biggest cities of Turkey, or even directly towards foreign countries, instead of heading first to the capital city of their native region.

Regional development

The greatest number of migrating people has headed to the three largest cities: between 1980 and 1990, the population of Ankara increased by 109 per cent, that of Istanbul by 82 per cent and that of Izmir by 65 per cent, while the overall urban population of Turkey grew by 64 per cent. The population of some cities in the south, the east and southeast almost doubled between 1980 and 1990.

Until the recent over-crowding of the three largest cities, the urban network of the regions was remarkably balanced between small, medium and large cities distributed over the whole country. Until the early 1980s the medium-size cities (100 000 to 500 000 habitants) were growing faster than the leading metropolitan areas. This trend seems, however, to have slowed down in the last five years. (Table 7)

Thrace (2.5 per cent), the Marmara and Aegean regions (4.4 per cent), and the Mediterranean region (3.7 per cent) are the coastal areas with the highest average annual population growth rates between 1970 and 1990, showing a total increase of about 90 per cent over the period. This is, of course, linked to the development of ports and industrial areas.

Settlement structure

Urban growth occurs in several ways, all accompanied by land speculation and increasing land and housing prices:

Table 7. **POPULATION OF TURKISH CITIES, trends**

Districts	Urban population, 1985 (million inhab.)	Trends (index 100 = 1980)		
		1980	1985	1990
Ankara	2.74	100	184	204
Antalya	0.40	100	137	198
Ordu	0.22	100	153	192
İçel (meisin)	0.57	100	142	190
Sauli Urfa	0.40	100	131	187
İstanbul	5.56	100	131	182
Gaziautep	0.64	100	128	168
İzmir	1.80	100	139	165
Van	0.19	100	119	165
Adana	1.14	100	133	162
Bursa	0.84	100	126	161
Diyarbakir	0.47	100	128	157
Tekirdag	0.20	100	121	154
Siirt	0.24	100	131	152
Sanisun	0.41	100	121	152
Denizli	0.25	100	125	150
Manisa	0.49	100	121	151
Aydun	0.30	100	122	144
Konya	0.41	100	124	144
Balikesi	0.41	100	121	139
Elazig	0.23	100	118	137
Kars	0.20	100	118	135
Tokat	0.25	100	120	137
Maidin	0.24	100	113	135
Trabzon	0.24	100	131	134
Kayseri	0.49	100	121	133
Eskiselir	0.40	100	118	133
Kühtaya	0.20	100	119	132
A. Karalisar	0.23	100	117	132
Sakarya	0.23	100	116	133
Kocaeli	0.41	100	120	131
Matay (Iskenderum)	0.43	100	114	131
K. Maraz	0.34	100	118	128
Erzurum	0.35	100	122	127
Siras	0.32	100	112	127
Turkey	**26.87**	**100**	**133**	**164**

Source: State Institute of Statistics, *Statistical Yearbook of Turkey* (1990) and *Environmental Statistics and Natural Resource Accounting in Turkey* (1991).

-- concentration in the old city centres; this process is accompanied by the overall destruction of older buildings for widening roads and modernising the city structure and houses;

-- illegal settlements spreading uncontrolled around the main Turkish towns but using village-type houses; these squatters often occupy the only green areas left in the suburbs of the giant cities of Istanbul, Ankara and Izmir. They are usually located on public land and have insufficient infrastructural facilities. The dwelling units are continuously improved by the squatters and provided with basic conveniences. In this way, suburbs expand unplanned;

-- coastal urbanisation caused by settlements of secondary houses gradually occupying a continuous land strip along the Marmara, Aegean and Mediterranean shores.

In the structure of cities, housing is also remarkably mixed with industrial buildings. Except for trade, which is a traditional activity of towns where specific areas are devoted to specific trades and handicrafts, industry expands uncontrolled. Until recently there were no "industrial zones" in Turkish towns. There are several active industrial areas where all kinds of productive activities are mixed with all kinds of housing.

3. Decentralisation

Until the 1980s, settlement planning was carried out and enforced at central government level. Although local authorities were given diversified responsibilities, such as the provision and operation of urban services, and implementation of physical plans and development control, the decision-making powers were exercised mainly by the central authority through the approval of plans, development regulations and programmes and finally through financial instruments.

The first step towards decentralisation was to strengthen the financial viability of local authorities through new legislation on municipal finance enacted in 1981. Today, contributions to municipalities from the national budget total just over 10 per cent while property taxes are now collected by the municipalities.

The second step towards decentralisation was the establishment of metropolitan authorities in three major cities (now extended to eight) and the transfer of decision-making powers with regard to physical planning to these authorities. In 1985, delegation of physical planning powers to all local authorities was initiated. Municipalities are assigned full responsibility for planning and implementation within their territories, with the exception of a few cases.

A reorganisation scheme was put into effect within the central government. The Ministry of Reconstruction and Resettlement was merged with the Ministry of Public Works to form the new Ministry of Public Works and Settlement. Among its duties are the setting of national guidelines, the planning at a macro level, the definition of planning standards and the training of municipal staff.

4. *Impact of urbanisation*

The most severe environmental impacts of urbanisation are manifested in **pollution from the domestic sectors**: domestic effluents, air pollution from household heating and domestic waste. Probably the most severe and most widespread are domestic wastewater discharges due to lack of sewerage infrastructure and treatment plants; illegal settlements accentuate this problem. Little improvement can be noted in this field.

Household heating is a major contributor to air pollution in most urban areas, but some improvements have been achieved by conversion from indigenous, highly polluting coal to natural gas.

Household waste disposal is another problem. At many locations refuse seems to be disposed of in a haphazard fashion, which can create sanitary and health problems. This also burdens the municipality with extra costs as refuse collection cannot be performed efficiently.

Pollution of a different kind is noise pollution by domestic activities. A well-known phenomenon of urban areas is the different social atmosphere compared to rural areas, where contact between people is more intense. In urban areas, this lack of contact with the neighbours can result in a social behaviour where consideration for the neighbours or the neighbourhood is weakened or non-existent. The construction of very large apartment blocks with little regard for the need to insulate or muffle the sound is a major contributor to the problem.

79

5. *Impact of economic growth*

The clearest sign of Turkey's rapid economic growth is the large number of industrial establishments, of all sizes, in and around Turkish cities.

Industrial air pollution is closely related to the increase in energy use in industry and to the growth of heavy industries. Recently established industries are subject to strict regulations regarding the installation of control equipment but old and, particularly state-owned, enterprises are not well regulated.

Industrial waste water discharges are major contributors to water pollution in urban areas and hence to pollution of urban coastal areas, rivers and soil. The development of industrial estates in recent years has helped to treat industrial discharges and thereby reduce their impacts.

Industrial waste, particularly hazardous waste, has grown proportionately with industrial production. Treatment facilities are minimal and their disposal is haphazard. They pose serious dangers for soil and ground water and in some cases for public health.

6. *Impact of income growth*

One of the indicators of personal income growth and overall economic development is the growth in transport and general mobility. In Turkey this is clear from the increase in car ownership and use, in public transport in urban areas and motor transport of goods. Traffic pollutes by means of exhaust fumes, noise, vibrations, and the spilling of oil and fuel, and endangers the safety of people.

Vehicle growth over the last 20 years was far higher in Turkey than in other OECD countries: almost 1 000 per cent for cars and almost 300 per cent for trucks. Given the relatively old age-structure of the vehicles and lack of effective pollution control, pollution growth in cities was also spectacular. Although regulations on new cars are at least at EC standards, lack of maintenance and spare parts means that their performance is poor (Table 8). Nevertheless the number of passenger vehicles per 100 persons is still relatively low: three in Turkey as compared to 29 in Spain and 49 in Germany.

Table 8. VEHICLES AND OWNERSHIP RATE, 1980-1990

	Passenger cars			Goods vehicles (a)			Vehicle Ownership, 1990 (veh./100 persons)
	(1000)		1980-1990 % change	(1000)		1980-1990 % change	
	1980	1990		1980	1990		
Turkey	742	1 885	154	331	823	149	3.3
Canada (b)	10 256	12 811	25	2 903	3 396	17	48.6
USA (b)	121 601	143 081	18	33 667	43 554	29	57.6
France (c)	19 250	23 550	22	2 457	4 670	90	41.6
w. Germany	23 192	30 695	32	1 277	1 409	10	48.7
Italy (b,c,d)	17 686	26 199	48	1 600	2 644	65	43.9
Spain	7 557	12 010	59	1 362	2 340	72	30.1

a) Goods vehicles data refer in principle to: vans, lorries (trucks), and road tractors.
b) 1989 data; % change refers to 1980-1989 period.
c) Goods vehicles do not include road tractors.
d) Goods vehicles include three-wheeled vehicles.

Source: OECD, IRF

II. CURRENT ENVIRONMENTAL STATUS AND FUTURE REQUIREMENTS

1. *Air pollution*

Air pollution by sulphur dioxide (SO_2) and particulate matter is severe in many urban centres. In the 1989-90 winter season, 11 cities exceeded the Turkish SO_2 limit value of 250g/m3(six-month average) and two exceeded the particulate limit value of 200g/m3(two-month average). The "short-term" SO_2 limit value of 400g/m3(24 hr average) was exceeded on more than 30 days in 12 cities and the equivalent particulate limit value of 300g/m3 was exceeded on more than 30 days in four cities (Figure 11 and Table 9). Several cities exceeded the EEC guidelines for the winter months (22 cities in 1988-89 and 24 in 1989-90). No data enable comparison with the WHO one-hour guideline of 350g/m3; it is likely, however, that in the most severely affected cities, guidelines would also be exceeded for most of the winter season and on a significant number of occasions in the "cleaner" summer season.

An additional air pollution load is imposed through **oxides of nitrogen, carbon monoxide** and **lead particulates** emitted from largely uncontrolled motor

Figure 11. URBAN AIR POLLUTION

City centres with high SO_2 and/or particulate matter concentrations during winter season

vehicle fleets together with the likelihood of organochlorines from the practice of stubble burning in adjacent agricultural areas.

Such high urban air pollution levels almost certainly result in an increased **morbidity amongst the city populations** with a concomitant increased load on medical and health services and decrease in labour productivity. The sources of air pollution are as follows.

Domestic heating

The widespread use of coal for domestic heating and hot water is a significant contributor to urban air pollution. Although the per capita use of coal for domestic heating has been relatively stable over the last ten years and, although the recent reticulation of natural gas through a number of large cities has the potential to reduce coal use, this must be set against a continuing increase in urban populations. Air quality will be adversely affected as long as coal burning dominates in heating of domestic premises: SO_2 controls and particulate controls are not feasible in domestic applications, as they are with large industrial users.

Table 9. AVERAGE CONCENTRATIONS OF SO$_2$ AND PARTICULATE MATTER, winter 1988/1989 and 1989/1990

Cities	Sulphur Dioxide				Particulate matter			
	Average concentration (a) (µg/m^3)		Number of days exceeding the short-term limit value (b)		Average concentration (c) (µg/m^3)		Number of days exceeding the short-term limit value (d)	
	1988/89	1989/90	1988/89	1989/90	1988/89	1989/90	1988/89	1989/90
Diyarbakir	197	491	20	89	186	289	39	91
Malatya	218	385	19	69	76	164	-	22
Bursa	313	385	42	64	99	154	14	22
Istanbul	266	356	83	131	149	161	40	53
Konya	182	309	14	42	95	106	6	11
Kütahya	47	299	-	48	79	113	1	3
Eskisehir	269	297	28	33	97	70	-	1
Sivas	319	296	64	66	124	149	25	5
Izmit	224	295	39	51	102	121	10	8
Ankara	271	268	-	-	128	152	-	-
Iskenderun	48	259	-	-	101	157	13	8
Samsun	139	246	6	21	57	60	-	-
Erzurum	154	244	48	45	128	131	3	37
Elazig	56	243	1	24	42	223	1	53
Canakkale	216	230	12	35	20	44	-	-
Yozgat	240	229	39	23	72	71	-	-
Usal	188	199	-	-	106	105	-	-
K. Maras	221	196	26	44	110	63	11	-
Kayseri	258	190	49	28	131	124	19	14
Gaziantep	223	177	-	-	142	126	-	-
Tekirdag	206	163	154	6	105	96	1	-
Kastamonu	307	157	45	11	121	76	1	1
Izmir	127	115	-	-	128	116	6	3
Kars	202	105	11	-	88	73	5	-
Zonguldak	120	101	-	-	134	147	21	24
Erzincan	..	170	..	10	..	166	..	26

a) Average sulphur dioxide, winter season: 250 µg/m^3 (Turkey), 125 µ/m^3 (WHO).
b) Sulphur dioxide short term: 400/µg/m^3 Turkey), 350 µ/m3 (WHO).
c) Average particulate matter, winter season: 200/µg/m3 (Turkey), 120 µ/m3 (WHO).
d) Particulate matter short term: 300 µ/m3 (Turkey), 350 µg/m3 (WHO).
Source: Turkish State Institute of Statistics, *Environmental Statistics - Air Pollution 1980-1990* (1992).

Industry

Industrial sources directly account for about 20 per cent of SO_2 emissions. When coupled with industrial demand for electricity, industry actually contributes directly and indirectly a little over 50 per cent of SO_2 emissions. Information is not available to estimate the industrial contribution to atmospheric particulates; however, it would be expected to be significant.

The use of coal as a fuel for small industries scattered throughout urban areas is a cause for concern, because such sources are not amenable to SO_2 control; as for particulate controls, they are unlikely to be sufficiently profitable and technical competence may be lacking to install and maintain them.

There appears to be widespread generation of "fugitive dust" from small industrial premises through the lack of simple dust-control measures such as covered conveyer belts, regular sweeping of sealed surfaces, failure to cover loads on trucks, spillage due to carelessness and the myriad simple "good housekeeping practices" which conserve valuable products and make for a tidy and well-run operation. Education and advice from pollution control inspectors can make major inroads in this source of air pollution whilst reducing costs for the operators through the prevention of wastage.

Power generation

About 60 per cent of total electricity consumption is generated in thermal power stations, half of which burn lignite coal with an average sulphur content of between 1.3 per cent and 3.5 per cent and occasionally much higher. Power generation accounts for approximately 55 per cent of the estimated total of SO_2 emissions.

The prohibition of use of high-sulphur lignite in the Ankara region in favour of imported low-sulphur lignites has reduced estimated SO_2 emissions from 50 000t/y to 15 000t/y. Such a dramatic reduction indicates what can be achieved by selection of cleaner fuels. The availability of large reserves of lesser quality indigenous lignites, however, warrants investigation of the feasibility of pre-treatment of such fuels to reduce sulphur content. Desulphurisation of flue gases to produce industrial grade sulphuric acid should be considered on some large power plants. For new power stations and those being re-equipped, consideration should be given to the use of fluid bed or pressurised fluid bed systems which are amenable to SO_2 control by limestone injection.

No statistics are available for the contribution by power generation to the emission of particulates. However, since many power stations do not have effective particulate control systems, it is likely that power generation accounts for up to 30 per cent of anthropogenic particulate matter in the air. Such uncontrolled particulate emissions are no longer acceptable practice and a control programme should be instituted. Any new thermal power stations must incorporate modern particulate controls to maintain emissions below 50mg/m3.

Thermal power plants currently contribute an estimated 17 per cent of the emissions of oxides of nitrogen (NOx). This relatively low figure probably reflects the low burning temperatures encountered in many lignite-burning plants. To avoid increasing this contribution through the development of new, more thermally efficient plants, attention needs to be given to the control of NO_x emissions by use of modern "low-NO_x" burners.

Mobile sources

Motor vehicles are estimated to contribute about 46 per cent of the NO_x emissions in Turkey and are undoubtedly a significant source of carbon monoxide, hydrocarbons and particulates. Yet it is currently estimated that in Istanbul only one person in seven owns a motor vehicle. This ratio is very low compared to other European countries and is bound to increase with the increasing affluence of the population. With increasing ownership will come increasing traffic congestion, air pollution and noise in cities unless convenient, efficient public transport systems are developed together with traffic management schemes to discourage individual use of the motor vehicle for commuter transport.

In coastal cities, shipping can contribute to air pollution through the burning of coal and through poorly maintained or operated oil burning boilers or diesel engines. The prohibition of coal burning vessels in Istanbul harbour should be strictly enforced and locally operated vessels regularly inspected for proper operation and maintenance.

Others

The open burning of rubbish and garden wastes in urban areas contributes to the air pollution load and can cause serious local deterioration in air quality through the burning of plastics.

In agricultural areas on the outskirts of some cities the practice of stubble or straw burning is a further contributor to air pollution. The practice generates

85

large quantities of particulate matter and may re-mobilise pesticides used on the crops to produce a more toxic smoke than would normally be expected. Discontinuation of this practice should be encouraged through education and advice from the Ministry of Agriculture.

2. Water pollution

Water supply and sewerage

Total water use for domestic purposes is estimated to be 4 million m3/d, which is equal to 70 l/capita/day.

An estimated 25 per cent of the overall population are connected to sewerage systems; this is equivalent to more than 50 per cent of the urban population. The service distribution within the urban population is as follows:

-- served by septic tanks   43 % (12.0 million)
-- served by latrines   1 % (0.3 million)
-- served by sewerage systems   56 % (16.0 million)
-- served by proper wastewater treatment 6 % (2.0 million)

Industrial waste waters

There is no general inventory of industrial waste waters and their load in Turkey. The total water use is estimated to be 3 million m3/d. The load can be estimated to be of the same order of magnitude as the household and municipal load, but due to toxic compounds, wastewater discharges are very harmful in some areas.

Industry represents a relatively high share of GDP. At present, manufacturing industry accounts for about 70 per cent of industrial value. The textile and leather industry is the most polluting; the chemicals industry, petrochemicals, fertilizers and pharmaceutical products have developed rapidly in recent years. Mining produces much chromium and mercury, which have heavy impacts on receiving water.

Major industrial polluters in the coastal areas are located as follows:

The Mediterranean and Aegean Seas   800 units
The Black Sea   150 units
The Sea of Marmara   900 units

Many of these industries are located in urban areas, such as those along the Sea of Marmara (Bursa, Izmit, Istanbul).

Some industrial plants have wastewater treatment facilities, but most of them do not function properly. The exact number, types and capacities of the treatment plants are not known.

Agricultural pollution

At present, 28 million hectares of land (35 per cent of the total land area) are under cultivation. Uncontrolled use of fertilizers and pesticides has caused environmental problems in the areas of intensive agriculture, such as the plains upstream of Adana and the Islanderum gulf.

Present state of pollution

No reliable data are available on the present total wastewater load. It might be in the order of 50 million PE [20-25 million population equivalent (PE) from communities and 25-30 million PE from industry]. The total BOD-load into the surface waters is estimated between 3 000 and 5 000 t/d. This means that the average input into the surface waters would be at least 10 mg/1, which in turn means strong pollution.

The overall state of pollution is not well identified because monitoring is inadequate, even if much progress has been made in this respect recently. The surface waters are widely polluted. Water pollution is mainly caused by untreated domestic waste waters as well as mostly untreated industrial waste waters, which also often contain toxic compounds.

The water resources in Turkey are generally abundant and this fact mitigates the state of pollution, but there are areas where water is scarce. On the other hand, a major part of Turkey's groundwater reserves for drinking water have been exploited and more and more surface waters have to be used for drinking water purposes. Economic and demographic growth as well as the lack of effective control on water resources are increasingly affecting the water quality in several areas in Turkey. For instance:

-- the İstanbul Region (Golden Horn, Bosphorus, the Sea of Marmara and İzmit Bay) is the most polluted area because of industrial and urban wastes;

-- Ankara Region (mainly urban wastes);

-- İzmir Bay (various industrial and urban wastes);

-- Porsuk River (various industrial and urban wastes);

-- Simav River (waste waters from boron mines);

-- Nilufer River (various industrial and urban wastes);

-- Sapanca Lake (planned to be used as a source of drinking water, but polluted by industrial wastes);

-- İznik Lake (heavily polluted);

-- Eber Lake (wastes from Afyon sugar and alkaloid factories);

-- Karamuk Lake (SEKA paper factory);

-- Burdur Lake (Keciborlu sulphur factory, sugar factory and milk factory).

Future requirements

The sustainable development of water resources requires proper wastewater treatment for communities and industrial plants. The investments needed for the construction of a sewerage system and a proper treatment in the future could be estimated from the following table including:

Year	1990 (millions)	2000	2010
Population	56	70	82
Urban population	34 (59%)	49 (70%)	55*
Population served by sewer systems	19	30*	45*
Water treatment	3.5	20*	45*

* Estimated as an indication of future requirements.

88

The table clearly shows that population growth and urbanisation already cause and will cause major future environmental problems unless massive investments are made in water sanitation facilities.

3. Noise pollution

The main sources of noise are: neighbours, road traffic, air traffic, construction work, rail traffic and industry.

As in most other countries, road traffic in Turkey is the main source of noise. Smaller towns are in general situated alongside a highway, and noise, especially from buses and trucks, is blanketing these towns. In the future this traffic should be guided around these towns. In the urbanised areas local traffic is becoming rapidly intensified and because of commuting by private car, traffic congestion is heavy every morning and evening. In urbanised areas it is not only necessary to improve public transport in quantity and in speed, but in addition the flow of private traffic has to be directed in such a way that its entry into the inner cities is prevented as much as possible. Already in 1976 the Environment Directorate of the OECD published the report *Evaluation of Traffic Policies for the Improvement of the Urban Environment*, which describes various methods of evaluation used to assess the impact of traffic policies on the urban environment. Maximum permissible sound levels at the facade of the houses should be introduced, and traffic planning should be used to obtain these set goals.

Air traffic creates noise mainly through take-off and landing operations. Though the latest generation of aircraft creates less noise, the number of planes in operation has risen. It is possible to minimise the noise pollution from air traffic by take-off and landing restrictions and the description of special flight paths. However, because of the high noise levels of aircraft, it is necessary to locate the airports away from built-up areas and to take proper steps, e.g. by land use planning, to prevent the construction of new buildings in noisy areas.

Construction work is by definition temporary. Still, the noise levels during construction can be high and cause much disturbance. The Turkish Noise Control Regulation allows the use of several types of equipment during the evening and the night and on holidays only if a special permit is secured from the municipality. The Noise Control Regulation sets limits on the noise levels from the construction site during daytime hours. Early in 1991 it was proposed to set noise limits on certain types of equipment in accordance with EC directives. Existing legislation should be enforced more often.

Rail traffic noise depends on the kind of drive being used -- the number of axles and the speed of the train. Rail traffic, contrary to highway traffic, is not to be considered a continuous source of noise and requires a different approach for noise abatement. At lower speed nuisance occurs where noisy diesel-driven locomotives are used. At higher speed the inter-action between wheels and rail creates high noise levels. As with aircraft noise land use planning should be used to prevent the construction of noise-sensitive buildings close to the railways.

Industrial noise is caused by large industries, by small industries inside residential areas and by small industries gathered at assigned locations at town borders. In general, when industries were started, the noise created by the working method used, the equipment and the tools was not considered. Alongside the consideration of noise when new industrial activities are started, an overall policy should be formulated which aims at the improvement of existing industrial technologies.

In Turkey neighbourhood noise has not yet been acknowledged as dangerous to health. Because there are so many other environmental threats, neighbourhood noise is presently disregarded. If neighbourhood planning and building quality are not improved in the short term, damage related to noise will be high as will the cost of retrofitting the buildings and renovating the neighbourhoods in the future. As a result, it is likely that if planning and building quality is not improved in the short term, there will be a large financial burden or a loss of invested capital because the renovation of these areas will be necessary in the near future.

4. *Soil pollution*

The contamination of the soil by urban and industrial activities is not well documented but can be seen in the everyday operation of small workshops and inferred from the use of septic tanks for waste disposal and from experience gained in other countries. The control of soil and groundwater contamination is essential to Turkey's on-going reliance on groundwater resources for potable water supplies.

Septic tanks

Although many soils act as an excellent filter medium to neutralise the biological and pathological contaminants in sewage waste, the build-up of nitrogen and phosphorous in the soil eventually exceeds its absorption capacity and these contaminants begin to leach into the groundwater -- perhaps decades after the use of septic tanks began. If the groundwater is used for human consumption, such contamination can have effects on health. If it flows into seas, rivers or lakes, it adds to the nutrient load and contributes to the process of eutrophication. Whereas the effects of a drain or pipe discharge will cease when the source is controlled, where the contaminants are stored in the soil and groundwater there may be little diminution of contaminant flow for decades after the source has been removed.

A firm policy should be established for the provision of reticulated sewerage and appropriate waste treatment for all communities over 20 000 persons. The developers of all new residential development areas in such communities should be required to install reticulated sewers and make an appropriate contribution to the headwork costs of eventual main sewers and treatment plants. When central sewerage reticulation is available it is then far less costly to connect the development, and the cost of housing properly reflects the cost of appropriate sewage collection and treatment.

Underground storage

Underground storage tanks, particularly those in filling stations for automotive fuel, are a notorious source of soil and groundwater pollution. Leakages which appear insignificant on a day-to-day basis may cause a build-up of contaminants in the soil and groundwater over time, which may be very difficult and costly to redress. In other countries, investigation of commonly installed, single-skin, steel underground fuel storage tanks has revealed a high proportion of leakage after 10 to 30 years, depending on soil conditions. The hydrocarbons and fuel additives, such as lead and chlorine compounds, can poison surrounding vegetation and seriously contaminate groundwater.

All new or replacement underground tanks used for storage of any materials other than potable water, should be double-skinned with a facility for testing the space between the skins for leakage. A programme should be established for the eventual upgrading of all underground storage tanks. In the longer term leak-proof tanks will provide a return on their costs through savings in lost raw materials or products.

Industrial contamination

In addition to the likely leakages from industrial use of underground storage tanks and pipelines, other potential sources of soil and groundwater contamination are: the storage of raw materials, products and waste materials directly on the ground; spillages from process operations and from materials handling systems entering drainage sumps; sludges containing contaminants from wastewater treatment plants disposed of by land dumping.

No matter how harmless stockpiles and waste dumps may appear to be, they should only be allowed on properly sealed and bunded areas with underdrainage for the detection of leakage or leachate. Such a facility, for the storage of chromium wastes, is in the process of construction at a plant in Adana. There is little information available, however, on storage practices in other industries.

The proliferation of small workshops throughout major urban areas is likely to be the cause of significant soil and groundwater contamination. The common practice of disposing of waste oil on the ground around such premises destroys vegetation and poses a threat of groundwater contamination by the oil itself, and by lead, toxic combustion products and other heavy metals and chlorinated hydrocarbons depending on the various additives in the original oil. The policy of aggregating such premises in planned industrial areas, where centralised waste collection facilities can be provided, is a positive step in controlling this problem.

As with the prevention of "fugitive dust", much can be done to reduce the potential for soil and groundwater contamination in industry by the application of "good housekeeping practices" -- overflow alarms on storage tanks, oil interceptors on drains, bunds around storage areas, immediate clean-up of spillage, provision of containers for storage of minor wastes, regular inspection and repair of pipes and valves, etc. A combination of education, demonstration and inspection by the control agency and by industry associations is possibly the most effective control mechanism.

5.   *Waste management*

Municipal

Quantities of municipal wastes in Turkey compare to quantities collected elsewhere in Europe on a per capita basis, although with less packaging waste. (Table 10)

Table 10. **AMOUNTS OF MUNICIPAL WASTES**

	Kg/cap	Composition of municipal wastes (%) [a]									
		Paper and cardboard		Plastics		Glass		Metals		Others	
	1989	1980	1985	1980	1985	1980	1985	1980	1985	1980	1985
Turkey	353	8.5	9.3	1.9	2.3	1.6	1.6	1.7	1.7	86.3	83.5
Canada	625	36.5	36.5	4.7	4.7	6.6	6.6	6.6	6.6	45.7	45.7
USA	864	29.7	34.7	5.3	6.7	10.3	9.0	9.6	8.8	45.1	40.8
France	303	28.0	27.5	6.0	4.5	11.0	7.5	5.0	6.5	50.0	54.0
w.Germany	318	19.9	17.9	67.1	5.4	11.6	9.2	3.9	3.2	58.5	64.3
Italy	301	22.5	22.3	6.8	7.2	6.7	6.2	2.9	3.1	61.4	61.6
Spain	322	15.0	15.0	6.0	6.0	6.0	6.0	2.5	2.5	70.5	70.5

a) Includes organic substances such as waste food; in Turkey cinder represents a large part
of municipal wastes (for example: in Istanbul, 42% in winter and 16.5% in summer;
32.4% in Ankara and 11% in Antalya over the full year).

Source: OECD.

The management and disposal of municipal wastes in Turkey varies greatly
across the country. Composting plants have been installed in some cities whilst
in other centres disposal practices vary from landfill to dumping in quarries,
streams and even the sea.

Firm policies on the management of municipal waste need to be developed
and technical support provided, particularly to communities of fewer than
100 000 people, to ensure that waste disposal practices do not threaten valuable
environmental or economic resources.

Although much material is recycled through "picking over" of waste in
street containers, an anticipated increase in urban affluence will result in the
phasing out of this practice and in a rapid change in both the nature and volume
of municipal waste unless precautionary measures are taken. Separation of
household waste at source, as practiced in the tourist resort near Bodrum, can
facilitate resource recycling and reuse. The recycling of glass practiced in
several cities, should be encouraged and expanded to other materials -- perhaps
by the imposition of a deposit system on all containers imported into or
manufactured in the country.

The glass manufacturing industry was established in Turkey only after the Republic itself. It is one of the fastest growing manufacturing industries in Turkey: its value added is estimated to grow annually by 9.3 per cent over the VIth Five-Year Development Plan Period; its share in the total exports of the country has also increased and is expected to reach 2.2 per cent in 1994.

A glass manufacturing industry's initiative

The glass manufacturing industry introduced a series of waste management measures in 1986. The Turkish Glass-Bottle Company (TGBC) initiated a campaign for the separate collection and reuse of waste glass, mainly from three large cities: Istanbul, Izmir, Bursa and their vicinities, aiming at collecting 25 000 tons of broken glass per year. This required initially:

- collecting and then transporting waste glass; medium-size containers owned by TGBC were installed in Istanbul, Bursa, and Izmir cities; lorries were assigned for their transport;

- constructing a waste-glass washing plant, put into operation in 1986.

Four types of collection systems

Today, there are four main types of collection systems:

i) Collection of waste glass in <u>Istanbul, Izmir and Bursa residential areas</u> through medium-size containers, owned and handled by TGBC; there are two different containers: one for white glass, and the other for green and amber-coloured glass.

ii)   Collection of waste glass from the solid waste <u>landfilling or disposal sites of Istanbul</u> and its vicinity by individuals or small companies.

iii) Handling and transfer of white, green and amber-coloured glass generated by the factories and warehouses of "Tekel", the state-owned enterprise manufacturing most alcoholic beverages in Turkey: separation and storage of broken glass is done by Tekel, whereas collection is done by TGBC.

iv)   Recycling of <u>broken glass generated in the glass manufacturing process</u> in the Pasabahçe Glass Factory, after washing.

The recovery target for broken glass was not achieved in the period 1986-1989, but it was achieved in 1990 with a total amount collected of 26 489 tons in the year (see figure).

Reuse of waste glass

Broken glass collected from various locations is transported to the TGBC waste-glass washing plant built in Istanbul in 1986 as mentioned earlier. The total amount of waste glass washed and recycled back into glass production is somewhat smaller than the amount collected, but reached almost 25 000 tons in 1990. Now, broken glass provides 15 to 60 per cent of the total raw material used in the company's operations.

A successful programme to be expanded

Thus the programme of waste glass collection and reuse has achieved its targets and allows substantial savings in raw materials for the glass industry. Efforts will be made to expand collection of waste glass all over Turkey, and to expand correspondingly the capacity for washing broken glass and thus achieve higher rates of glass recycling.

Industrial

Industrial solid waste is stored in waste disposal dumps, mixed with municipal waste in landfill sites or, in some cases, used as a fertilizer or for soil improvement. There is little information available on the extent to which industrial solid waste disposal practices are impacting on soils and groundwaters.

Each industry should be held responsible for the disposal of its solid waste in a manner which does not threaten environmental or economic resources. Methods proposed for solid waste disposal should be an integral part of environmental impact assessment of new industrial proposals, and of environmental management plans for all existing factories.

The recycling of industrial wastes can be encouraged if organisations such as the Chambers of Industry establish waste exchange inventories to facilitate the use of one industry's waste as a raw material or process chemical for another.

Hazardous

The management of hazardous wastes in Turkey, as in many other industrialised countries, is inadequate to ensure proper handling and treatment. The lack of clear jurisdiction has encouraged attempts to circumvent the laws forbidding the importation of hazardous wastes. Although there are examples of such attempts having been foiled, it is likely that some hazardous wastes are entering the country undetected and that locally generated hazardous wastes are being disposed of or stored under unsatisfactory conditions.

The examples of clean-up programmes in the United States and the Netherlands, for instance, clearly show that timely action can avoid severe dangers and high costs in the future. Legal sanctions themselves, no matter how rigorously enforced, are not sufficient to discourage the improper storage and disposal of hazardous wastes; they must be coupled with other management tools; the generation of hazardous wastes must be minimised; and facilities must be available for proper storage and disposal of hazardous wastes.

The **minimisation of the generation of hazardous wastes** has been embodied in Turkish laws governing this issue. The policy can be strengthened by the application of the mechanisms outlined for the management of industrial waste generally: the full implementation of environmental impact assessment for new proposals; the requirement that waste management programmes be prepared and implemented by existing industries; and the encouragement of waste re-use.

The second requirement - the establishment of **proper storage and disposal facilities** - is recognised as being more difficult to implement. Governments in several other countries are currently wrestling with the issue and some of those with existing facilities are facing increasing community demands for their removal. The issue must be faced, however, since although modern industrial processes are tending towards the generation of fewer and fewer hazardous wastes, such wastes will be a continuing feature of industrial activity for many years. Furthermore, the clean-up of many contaminated sites is not possible until the recovered materials can be properly dealt with. Progress may best be made by drawing together government, industry and non-government environmental groups to develop a tripartite approach.

Medical

Medical wastes have, for many years, required special treatment to guard against the spread of infectious material. The traditional disposal methods of on-site incineration or immediate cover in landfill sites are less effective against some of the materials used in modern medical procedures. Some cytotoxic agents, for instance, must be incinerated at temperatures of 1000 degrees C or more to ensure full destruction. Such temperatures are seldom achievable in incinerators attached to smaller regional hospitals. Other medical procedures make use of radioactive substances which require appropriate handling, storage and eventual disposal.

All hospitals, medical centres and individual medical practices should have access to facilities for collection and disposal of medical waste appropriate for the medical procedures being used.

III. ASSESSMENT OF POLICIES

1. *Urban pollution control and prevention in the context of sustainable development*

The government of Turkey has adopted sustainable development as an overall environmental policy objective. It has also set standards which are consistent with such a policy objective. It is generally accepted that pollution prevention and control in urban areas have to be an integral part of the overall strategy of sustainable development. This implies that standards (both emission and ambient) are set and achieved in line with the long-term conservation of environmental and natural resources.

AIR POLLUTION PREVENTION IN ANKARA

AVERAGE CONCENTRATION OF AIR POLLUTANTS DURING THE WINTER SEASON
in $\mu g/m^3$

	Winter Season	Oct	Nov	Dec	Jan	Feb	Mar	Average
Particulates	1985-86	71	127	211	143	150	166	146
	1990-91	88	138	112	128	92	72	105
SO_2	1985-86	74	170	285	295	303	274	233
	1990-91	97	243	256	290	238	146	211

Severe air pollution levels

For several decades, rapid growth has resulted in high population and building density in the Ankara urban area. Severe air pollution by particulate matters and sulfur dioxide concentrations is recorded in the city. It is among the worst situations recorded in any city in the OECD countries. This is due to:

- insufficient heating infrastructures and the low quality of fuels used in individual heating systems;
- specific and unfavourable topographic and meteorological conditions.

In addition, exhaust gases emitted from urban transportation sources contribute to CO_2, CO, NO_x and VOC pollution.

Facing pollution from heating

Ankara Provincial Public Health Board is responsible for taking measures to improve air quality such as: specifying the operating conditions of heating systems, setting target ambient concentrations of pollutants as well as alarm levels, defining measures to be taken when these levels are exceeded, and establishing regulations concerning the types of fuels to be distributed in Ankara, such as liquid fuels with low sulphur content (from the Izmit refinery).

The Ankara Metropolitan Municipality has also taken the following measures to combat air pollution from heating:

- 50 000 houses and similar buildings had been converted to a natural gas heating system by end 1990. This figure increased to 110 000 by mid 1991 and is expected to reach 250 000 by the end of the project; 80 per cent of these conversions were achieved in high-pollution areas. The combustion of natural gas instead of coal or liquid fuels eliminates SO_2 , particulates, hydrocarbons, and CO emissions and further reduces emissions of NO and of CO_2; it is anticipated that, in the 1991-92 heating season, the following emissions will be prevented: 7 200 tons of sulphur dioxide, 5 400 tons of particulate matter, 1 400 tons of hydrocarbon, 1 400 tons of carbon monoxide, 435 000 tons of carbon dioxide;

- High quality coal was imported from South Africa and Soviet Union in the 1990-91 season, and the dust of this coal was cleaned off before distribution;
- Environmental inspectors from the Municipal health authority control the pollutant concentration continuously in order to determine whether or not pollutants in the air exceed the limits of: 400 $\mu g/m^3$ for sulphur dioxide, 300 $\mu g/m^3$ for particulate matters. If the limits are exceeded, special measures are taken. The same inspectors check up on fuel-transporting vehicles and buildings as well, since it is forbidden to sell, store, transport, distribute or use any fuel in Ankara except solid fuel imported by the Metropolitan Municipality of Ankara and liquid fuels supplied by the General Directorate of Petroleum from the Izmit Refinery;
- The training of professionals to install and maintain central heating systems is carried out through 9 public training centres in Ankara;
- All industrial establishments and high capacity central heating systems must obtain permits for heating operations.

Complementary measures

Firstly, exhaust gas emissions from vehicles are under the responsibility of the National General Directorate of Highways and of the Provincial Directorate of Traffic. In co-operation with the Middle East Technical University, the Municipality of Ankara has carried out projects to reduce emissions from buses by use of natural gas and exhaust emission control devices. Currently some of the buses are operating on natural gas.

Secondly, mass public transportation is deemed essential: 51 per cent of intra-urban transportation is supplied by Municipality buses and minibuses. In addition, the Ankara Metro and the Ankara Light Rail are under construction: the first 15 km of the Ankara Metro will be completed in 1995 and 500 000 passengers will be transported daily. The full 55 km of the Ankara Metro will be completed by 2015. The Ankara Light Rail will be 8.5 km long by 1993 and will transport 300 000 passengers daily.

Thirdly, parks and other urban green spaces produce oxygen and absorb carbon dioxide, absorb particulate matter and contribute to air circulation by creating heat differences in the air. Therefore, 500 000 trees are to be planted in the city each year from 1990 onwards, according to the Ankara Afforestation Plan.

Lastly, considering the direct relationship between air quality and energy efficiency, many projects aiming at energy saving are carried out by the Municipality with emphasis on thermal insulation of buildings and solar energy use.

Data available for pollution trends in urban areas of Turkey are very limited but it is obvious at this stage that neither emission levels, nor ambient quality, nor emission trends are consistent with sustainable development, particularly in large urban areas. Does this imply that irreversible changes on a large scale are occurring in Turkey? The answer is probably no; but to bring back some of the areas to the quality specified by legislation will be extremely costly and therefore will require a major effort at all levels over a considerable period of time.

Experiences of OECD countries show that municipalities in combination with central government can improve the urban environment through a whole range of policies: **urban planning, housing policies, urban conservation, environmental enhancement, infrastructure provision, urban economic policies, traffic, waste management and recycling, energy management and nature conservation**. Considerable efforts such as rehabilitation of housing units, reduction of pollution, conservation of architectural quality have also been targeted at upgrading inner city areas.

References have been made to some of the measures taken in Turkey concerning planning and pollution control. There is also a well developed housing policy, often in conflict, however, with conservation and environmental enhancement. There are three other areas where municipal authorities need to make greater effort and develop appropriate policies:

-- **Waste minimisation and recycling** is largely an urban responsibility and an urban problem. Turkish municipalities need to upgrade their waste collection, recycling and disposal services. As recently as the early 1980s there was a shortage of waste collection equipment. There is little effort to encourage waste minimisation in enterprises and successful waste recycling efforts could be developed further concerning waste from both households and small enterprises. Finally there is a lack of proper treatment and disposal.

-- **Transport in urban areas** is a major environmental and economic issue and the growth of urban traffic substantially exceeds the OECD average of 5 per cent in recent years. Urban traffic, apart from that in Ankara and Istanbul, moves at a relatively fast pace; but it is the second largest source of urban air pollutant. All public transport is in the form of buses which are relatively cheap and plentiful. As part of city planning, urban traffic management and road planning are in operation; pedestrian zones have been created but they are few. However most efforts go towards improving traffic flows; environment is still only a marginal concern of traffic planning and policies.

-- **Urban energy use** is a significant part of total national energy consumption (between 35 and 40 per cent in Turkey) and a major source of urban pollution. Over the last 20 years most OECD countries have introduced conservation strategies with explicit urban design. One of the major beneficiaries of such strategies was the environment in the form of reduced air pollution. Such programmes cover the residential, commercial and industrial sector. Such programmes could be further developed in Turkey with significant economic and environmental benefits.

2. *Implementation*

A second major issue concerning pollution prevention and control in urban areas is implementation. The legal frameworks, and in some instances detailed regulations, are available in Turkey to implement most of the essential elements of integrated pollution control. Provision has been made in the Environment Law for an environmental fund into which industries must pay fees which reflect their pollution potential; a proportion of pollution fines is paid into the environment fund and to municipalities; the principles of environmental impact assessment have been written into law; special incentives are available to encourage industries away from heavily urbanised and industrialised areas; the citizens of some communities are being required to contribute to the capital costs of sewage treatment.

There is little evidence, however, of any integration of this powerful legal framework either at central government or municipal level. Many different laws are involved and where any action is being taken, responsibility is not clear and there appears to be little accountability of either industry or government agencies. The causes are many:

-- lack of presence of the Environment Ministry in urban areas;

-- authorities in urban areas often favour short-term economic development over pollution control;

-- lack of finance for water treatment and sewage treatment;

-- inability of the municipalities to enforce pollution control concerning government and municipal enterprises;

-- inability of central and local authorities to control the construction of illegal settlements which are left without sanitation services.

These factors are present to various degrees in all urban areas and they often represent a combination of forces that prohibit the implementation of pollution control policies.

In addition to these institutional difficulties other factors also contribute to the weak implementation of pollution prevention and control policies:

-- **The effectiveness of instruments used for implementation is limited**. Regulatory instruments are insufficiently enforced and penalties for failure to comply with regulations are weak. They can be too low and then it is more profitable to pollute and pay the penalty; state enterprises are not prosecuted for not paying the penalty.

-- **Land-use planning** is the most important instrument for preventive policies in urban areas. It is widely used in Turkey and is prescribed by law. Its effectiveness is limited by the high growth rate of urban areas and by illegal settlements. Some of these factors, including immigration from rural areas to urban areas, are outside the powers of municipal authorities and only policies by the government can reduce pressure in urban areas. Land property rights are not very well defined and land use planning would receive better public support if these rights were clarified and if land registers were prepared and were made available to the public.

-- **Investment in public infrastructure** is essential for effective environmental policy. Under Law 3030, municipal infrastructure in the metropolitan municipalities is well co-ordinated between the various municipal authorities according to environmental needs. However, financial resources are far from sufficient and the investment rate is falling behind growing requirements. Allocation of central government funds for basic needs, such as a sewerage system, is not given high priority in the central planning process. Lack of proper sewerage systems in large and small cities is a danger to public health and, in some areas, hinders the development of tourism.

However, efforts have been made in urban areas with prevention policies which are likely to produce significant benefits for the future. Such measures include settlement planning, as practiced for example in the Metropolitan Municipality of İzmir, development of communal transport systems, and the use of clean fuels e.g. natural gas. Planning is also taking place at the larger regional levels, for instance to locate industries outside built-up areas, or to develop satellite towns with some autonomy next to main population centres. There is also some success in the implementation of the 1983 Environment Law concerning **new industrial installations** requiring appropriate pollution control equipment; but proper operation of the pollution control equipment should be monitored.

3.   *Financing*

Information on pollution control expenditures and their funding is not collected in a systematic way and is not readily available. Some data on governmental funding of water and sewage treatment investment are available at the Central Government level as are some additional data both on financing sources and on expenditures in the Metropolitan Municipalities. Given this lack of information an assessment of financing must be based on secondary sources.

The bulk of environmental expenditures comes from central government funding, where investment funds are allocated either to the Metropolitan Municipalities or to the Ministry of Public Works and Settlement or to the Bank of Provinces. This allocation of funds is carried out by the State Planning Organisation on the basis of the investment requirement submitted by the individual agencies. The SPO weighs economic and social requirements, such as environment, and is in fact the deciding power for public investment in the field of water supply and pollution control. Until recently water and sewerage charges were insufficient to repay central government funding: interest charges were not included and were based on historical costs. Consequently it was not possible to establish revolving funds that could be at least partially self-financing. More recently charges were increased to cover operation and maintenance as well as a substantial part of investment costs.

Local financing is complex and also far from sufficient to generate funds for environmental purposes. For example from pollution charges imposed by the municipalities, they can retain only 20 per cent; revenue allocation from central government collections amount to only 5 per cent of all taxes collected by the municipalities; real estate taxes, based on minimum values established by the government and revalued only every four years are out of date with inflation of 60 per cent per annum. Financing by industrial establishments is not documented at all. However it is generally argued that government-owned enterprises, most of them old and loss-making, cannot afford to finance pollution control expenditures and have to rely on governmental subsidies. As for private

103

industrial establishments they probably could afford to finance their pollution control operation if the regulations were enforced. On the whole the current system of financing is unfavourable to local financing of environmental expenditures, and not well enforced.

Given the difficult budgetary situation of the Central Government, and the weak revenue-raising capacity of local governments, the following financing methods are suggested:

-- more reliance needs to be placed on **service charges** for publicly provided environmental services;

-- reviewing the tax obligations of illegal settlers; at the moment illegal settlers are not paying local taxes (as distinct from some service charges) until their construction is legalised. Yet local governments are obliged to undertake expenditures on their behalf (e.g. road works) and to cope with certain types of pollution generated by them (e.g. air pollution, sewage discharge) without receiving any revenues in exchange;

-- more use of borrowing from international institutions; the SPO, together with the Undersecretariat for Treasury and Foreign Trade and the Ministry of Finance, is the main agency in approving **international borrowing** by municipalities for sewerage treatment, as in the case of the Metropolitan Municipality of İzmir with the World Bank;

-- use of public-private partnership, to associate funds from the business community, the non-profit sector, and international private firms.

Environmental **subsidies** are to be used only to a limited extent, under the acceptable exceptions to the Polluter-Pays-Principle. For instance it might be necessary to provide subsidies for retrofitting some non-profitable state enterprises which cannot be closed for reasons of regional unemployment. However, some government subsidies presently used for purposes of industry or tourism development are damaging for the environment and economically inefficient. These funds could be more efficiently used for financing environmental infrastructures.

4. *Environmental impact assessment*

Environmental impact assessment is a potentially powerful tool in environmental management. To realise its potential, however, it must embody some fundamental principles:

104

-- it must be applied to all proposals (developmental, policy and fiscal) which have potential for significant environmental effects;

-- the environmental significance of a proposal should be a matter for determination by the environmental agency but responsibility for referring a proposal should be with the proponent, in the first place. This can be achieved by a two-stage referral process: an initial brief description of the proposal and its anticipated environmental impact, followed by an appropriate level of environmental impact assessment as determined by the environmental agency;

-- the environmental impact assessment should be undertaken by the proponent or by competent consultants on its behalf, at the proponent's cost;

-- the environmental agency should have the power to determine the scope of the assessment and to require more, or more detailed, investigation;

-- evaluation of the environmental impact assessment should be undertaken by the environmental agency, with provision for public input into that process;

-- the actions necessary to implement the findings of the environmental impact assessment and the evaluation by the environmental agency, must be able to be legally enforced upon the proponent or other government agency after appropriate consultation.

Most of these features are contained in the existing Turkish environmental impact assessment law. The main impediment to implementation of the law appears to be the need to predetermine the range of activities which are to be subject to environmental impact assessment.

This impediment has arisen elsewhere, where such a predetermination has been attempted, and such a prescriptive approach has caused problems when a previously unforeseen, but environmentally significant, proposal has arisen. Another disadvantage of the prescriptive approach is that it is difficult to take account of the variation in sensitivity of different environmental systems -- a small wastewater treatment plant discharge may be of little environmental significance in a large well flushed river but may be the cause of catastrophic eutrophication in an already highly stressed enclosed bay or lake.

The benefit of a prescriptive approach is that it provides a clear guide to proponents as to what range of proposals is likely to generate the need for environmental impact assessment. If used, however, such an approach must be coupled with some reserve power to enable environmental impact assessment to be required for non-prescribed proposals on a case-by-case basis.

Whatever the mechanism chosen, there is an urgent need to bring the environmental impact assessment process into operation. This action should be closely followed by the introduction of a requirement for all existing industries and undertakings with a potential for causing environmental degradation, to develop legally binding environmental management programmes to the satisfaction of the environmental agency.

IV. RECOMMENDATIONS

1. *Sustainable cities*

The heavy concentrations of people living and working in urban areas make large cities all over the world the pressure points of the interface between economic development and the environment. It is here that a nation's policies for physical planning, housing, pollution prevention and control are subjected to their severest test.

Turkey, more than most other OECD countries, is a country where urban drifts will continue to be significant for a considerable time to come. This will pose a major challenge to the Turkish authorities, but it also provides a unique opportunity for imaginative policies to implement the **sustainable cities** concept which is a component of the Government's sustainable development strategy.

While many of the recommendations in this report are based on the lessons learned in OECD countries, there is only little guidance to be obtained from the experiences of other countries on the implementation of the still new sustainable cities concept.

Turkey could set an example to the world by adopting a holistic framework that would encompass the economic, social and environmental aspect of government policy; physical planning, housing, transport, urban air and water quality issues, and integrated pollution control would all be addressed so that policies would become mutually reinforcing rather than detracting from each other.

106

The sustainable cities concept is more than just a question of better integration or better resourcing; it is a new vision that should ultimately lead to cities that are better adapted to human needs than those which exist today.

The sum total of the recommendations that follow does not and cannot yet add up to this new vision of the future shape of our cities. This chapter's first recommendation must therefore be that the Turkish Government explore the meaning of the sustainable cities concept in the Turkish context. The OECD Group on Urban Affairs is already engaged in work on the role of cities in sustainable development and this material would provide a starting point for finding suitable responses for Turkish cities.

2. Institutional framework

Chapter 2 on Water Resource Management presented three different scenarios for institutional change in environmental management in Turkey. The assessment made in this chapter of the environmental problems of urban areas reinforces the conclusion that a single agency should be given the responsibility and accountability for all environmental matters. This again suggests that either scenario 2 or 3 is to be preferred to the first one.

Specific tasks could be delegated from that single agency (i.e. either the Regional Directorate of the Ministry of the Environment or the Regional Environment Authority) to local authorities where this does not create a conflict between a municipality's role in economic development and the enforcement of environmental regulations. In all cases local authorities should be accountable to the central agency as well as to the local population.

National policies, guidelines and goals which must be met by local authorities within established time frames should be defined. Failure to meet performance criteria adequately must be subject to some kind of censure by the authorities responsible.

3. Environmental impact assessment

The assessment of the likely environmental effects of new development proposals is an essential tool in maintaining the quality of the environment. The already prepared legislation for environmental impact assessment should be completed and implemented as a matter of urgency, at least for all major industrial, energy and tourism developments and for proposals for land-use changes involving substantial areas of land. Environmental impact assessment should be closely co-ordinated with central and local planning systems and the resulting land-use zoning should be strictly enforced to separate major industrial activities from residential uses.

4. *Pollution control programme*

The present pollution control programme needs to be extended to embody a number of new features. Policies are to be developed at a national, regional or local level to enforce specific practices such as prohibition of coal burning in domestic premises in cities or provision of sewerage reticulation by developers of new housing estates. Environmental impact assessment of all developments with a potential for causing significant pollution are to be developed including site suitability assessment and risk assessment.

Specific measures need to be taken concerning industry:

-- **New industrial projects** should be required to meet national guidelines for waste discharge and to use all reasonable and practicable measures to reduce the discharge of wastes below those guidelines. All existing industries should be required to develop programmes for the reduction of waste discharges within national guidelines and within specified and enforceable timeframes. Where the government owns and operates industrial enterprises it should set the example by applying the rules it lays down for private enterprise.

-- Engineering details of all proposed industrial projects need to be assessed to ensure that pollution control mechanisms are adequate, and that environmental management plans are prepared describing how the environmental impacts of the proposal will be minimised and managed. All industrial premises should be licensed with the conditions of such licenses establishing minimum pollution control performance and self-monitoring requirements; failure to comply with license conditions must be subject to penalties, severe enough to discourage malpractice. The recycling of industrial wastes can be encouraged through organisations such as the Chambers of Industry establishing waste exchange inventories to facilitate the use of one industry's waste as a raw material or process chemical for another.

As part of resource and waste management policies a number of new measures could be taken such as:

-- The conservation of valuable resources, particularly those which are non-renewable, should be encouraged by the promotion of low resource-use technologies and materials recycling. A deposit system applied to packaging items would encourage recycling and reduce demands on existing waste disposal sites.

-- All new or replacement underground tanks used for storage of any materials other than potable water should be double skinned with a facility for testing the space between the skins for leakage. A programme should be established for the eventual upgrading of all underground storage tanks. In the longer term leak-proof tanks will provide a return on their costs through savings in lost raw materials or products.

Pollution control inspectorates should be created to regulate and provide technical advice to industry and the public. A mechanism should also be put in place for ensuring that the costs of undertaking and administering pollution control are borne by those wishing to use some element of the environment for the disposal of their wastes; for instance industries should undertake or fund the studies necessary for environmental impact assessment.

5. *Urban environment*

A greater part of the **cost of providing services** to industrial or housing developments should be borne by the developer. All new housing developments should be required to provide a sewerage system within their boundaries and to make a "headworks contribution" consistent with the demand that the development will eventually make on the reticulated system.

A firm policy should be established for the provision of reticulated sewerage and appropriate waste treatment for all communities over a given size, such as 20 000 persons. The developers of all new residential development areas in such communities should be required to install reticulated sewers and make an appropriate contribution to the headworks costs of eventual main sewers and treatment plants. When central sewerage reticulation is available it is then far less costly to connect the development, and the cost of housing properly reflects the cost of appropriate sewage collection and treatment.

The use of septic tanks for sewage disposal should be phased out in urban areas close to seas, rivers, streams, wetlands and underground water. This might be encouraged by a "once-off" special charge against households to ise capital,

URBAN REHABILITATION: THE GOLDEN HORN OF ISTANBUL

A critical environmental situation within the city

The Golden Horn is a 7.5 km long water inlet in the very heart of İstanbul. It is about 1 km wide at its entrance into the Bosphorus strait and gradually narrows down to one hundred meters as it curves northwards to the mouths of the Alibeyköy and Kagithane rivers. This location explains its value for commercial shipping as well as for military purposes. Its shores have been the scene of great development during the last hundred years, with major industrial, commercial and harbour activities. In 1976, for instance, 11.3 million tons were transported by sea in the Golden Horn, six times the capacity of two other harbours of İstanbul: Haydarpaşa and Salipazari. With the growing but unplanned concentration of activities, the Golden Horn became a dense industrial slum, surrounded upstream by crowded settlements lacking sanitation facilities. Most of the buildings were blocking the urban landscape of the multi-century old city; some of them had been built illegally on landfills and were therefore quite unsafe. As water and air pollution increased, the lack of infrastructure, the lack of control and unchecked land erosion led to critical environmental conditions: the concentration of organic and chemical pollutants was so great that the whole district had become highly hazardous.

In the late 1970's:

- 200 000 tons/day of industrial liquid waste were discharged into the Golden Horn, of which 67 per cent were chemicals;

- 50 000 tons/year of industrial solid waste were discharged directly into the waters;

- 100 000 m³/day of untreated domestic wastes were discharged into the Golden Horn;

- air pollution levels in the area were above the maximum standards during more than six months a year.

The rehabilitation project: displacing polluting industries and remodeling the landscape

The Golden Horn Project, launched in 1984 by the Metropolitan Municipality of İstanbul and modified in 1989, dealt with the rehabilitation of the southern and northern coastal strips of the Golden Horn. It aimed at controlling effluent discharges and at landscaping. Within two years, most industrial and harbour structures, as well as slums, were eliminated from the shorefront of the Golden Horn. Expropriations and resettlements freed 90 hectares (235 acres); 400 000 people living in substandard dwellings were transferred to more salubrious housing outside the area; almost half of this area was converted into lawns and historical buildings were restored. 2 488 industrial and commercial settlements were relocated on industrial sites outside İstanbul, mostly on the Marmara sea shores, west of the city; relocation of these activities generated increased productivity and better control of emissions of pollution and wastes.

The Golden Horn itself was dredged: 450 000 m³ of bottom silt were extracted in 1986 and dumped into the deepest part of the Marmara sea. A comprehensive plan for collection, treatment and discharge of the liquid wastes generated by the remaining industrial and commercial activities as well as by the 4 million people living on the 16 500 ha of the watershed of the Golden Horn, was designed as part of the Greater İstanbul Sewerage Master Plan. The southern Golden Horn project comprises 11 km of open-cut interceptors and a 6.5 km tunnel interceptor. After treatment of about 864 000 m³/day, liquid wastes will be discharged into the bottom currents of the Marmara sea, 1 180 m offshore. The northern Golden Horn project includes a 17 km collector system, treatment stations, pumping units and discharge pipes into the Bosphorus at a point 70 meters deep .

The total cost of the project (as estimated in 1987) was US$ 300 million (of which US$ 120 million for expropriation costs alone). Funds are provided by the national and municipal budgets and by international loans and credits (e.g. World Bank).

Present state of the project

Urban rehabilitation operations have been conducted successfully and in a relatively short time span. The implementation of the pollution reduction and control system has progressed but is not yet completed. Although waters in the Golden Horn receive far fewer effluents, they are still being polluted by untreated effluents from urban and industrial sources, mainly shipyards and the textile industry. Some controversy persists among scientists and engineers about the environmental impacts of these measures; in addition, the implementation of water sanitation for the Golden Horn needs to be completed as part of a broader set of water sanitation projects for the 15 municipalities of İstanbul -- including the construction of a network of collectors and of several waste-water treatment plants -- in order to address the overall sanitation problems of the İstanbul metropolitan area and its rapidly increasing population and economy. The implementation of these projects has benefited from the creation of İSKİ (the İstanbul Water Supply and Sewerage Directorate) as the main authority in charge of co-ordinating and commissioning engineering work.

These projects also provide a core for the shaping of an environmental policy in the İstanbul urban area, and a key element of the area's master plan.

and an ongoing sewer rate for all households regardless of whether they discharge to the sewer or not.

Rehabilitation of inner city areas should be a priority of urban management and be implemented with environmental enhancement as the major objective.

Motor vehicles are significant contributors to urban air and noise pollution. The impact of the motor vehicle should be limited by the introduction of **efficient and attractive public transport** systems, the regulation of traffic flows through road system design and the enforcement of noise and exhaust emission controls to EEC standards. The latter would be assisted by the introduction of lead-free petrol throughout the country at the same or lower price as leaded fuel.

Urban authorities should develop and implement their own energy efficiency programme with specific environmental objectives. The burning of coal and oil should be phased out in preference to gas and solar energy in major urban centres. This change in fuel use is occurring in some centres but needs to be accompanied by a reduction in per capita energy use, encouraged by the provision of subsidies for the installation of modern, high efficiency boilers, more energy-efficient building design and household insulation.

6. *Financing*

Financing of environmental investment and other environmental expenditure should be a joint responsibility of central and local governments. Significantly more use should be made of **charges and taxes** by local authorities, such as pollution charges, penalties, user charges for environmental services, special energy charges and development taxes on land. The government should support these financing measures with necessary legislation. The receipts from these locally collected revenues should be retained by the municipalities and paid into environmental/conservation funds to be used for environmental protection.

The stringent budgetary conditions and the limited finance-raising ability of local government further suggests that new and sizeable ways to finance environmental infrastructure have to be found. Firstly, **international lending** institutions might extend their funding of environmental projects presented by central and local authorities.

Secondly, the lessons and successes of **public/private partnerships** in infrastructure financing or in school-building financing could be extended to environmental investments. The experience of Turkey and other OECD countries shows that these partnerships may take many different forms ranging from relatively informal joint working arrangements to formally constituted joint ventures. The partners involved can vary, but they are usually drawn from the government, business and non-profit sectors. Public/private partnership between international consortiums and central and local governments could also bring much-needed financing for environmental infrastructure, as well as technical know-how and management capabilities when necessary. (see chapter 5)

7. *Training and education*

The trend towards a greater decentralisation of environmental management brings with it a concomitant need for a decentralisation of environmental expertise. The massive investments and related actions needed for environmental protection in Turkey imply a variety of qualifications for policy making, administration, planning, design, construction, operation and maintenance, monitoring, etc. Turkey already has an excellent educational infrastructure which, if it is given the resources, will no doubt be able to provide the required training and education to staff at all levels.

It is also recommended that key texts elaborated by international organisations such as the OECD, World Bank, UNEP or UNESCO be translated.

Chapter 4

COASTAL ZONE MANAGEMENT

Coastal zones are some of Turkey's most valuable economic and environmental assets. The fact that the country's major economic growth centres are located in these zones, which form a 20-to-40-kilometer band along the coasts, exerts a magnetic force on the country's inhabitants, particularly those from Central and Eastern Anatolia. This is reflected in a sharp increase of population density in the coastal areas. The natural and economic profile of Turkey's coastal areas and the comparative advantages they offer for different types of economic development require an integrated approach to environmental protection. Economic activities concentrated in these areas include: agriculture; a range of industries; tourism; fishing; aquaculture; various modes of land, sea and air transport; and urban development.

The intensity and range of these economic activities impact heavily on the fragile coastal environment and its natural resources. Environmental impacts, which vary in character and intensity, range from low level discharge of untreated waste water to major alterations to the coastal landscape.

The Turkish coastline is rich in natural and environmental resources. The immense range of natural beauty and cultural attractions reflects the classical and post-classical history of the eastern Mediterranean, Anatolia and southeastern Europe. These resources include: unique coastal ranges (including karst areas); natural parks; fertile plains; coastal waters of different seas; waterways with many bays; and estuaries which possess highly valuable wetlands. Compared with other areas of Turkey, the coastal zones require a much higher degree of sustainable management in order to maintain their economic productivity while preserving their environmental quality.

Turkey has accepted that sustainable development should be the guiding principle for economic and environmental management; this means, among other

115

things, that today's development must be equitable to future generations. In practical terms, the management of environmental resources needs to be conducted in such a way as to protect human health and minimize the impact of development on existing ecological systems, ensuring, at the very least, their capacity to recover. Environmental management should also prevent pollution from causing economic damage and ensure that natural resources are never depleted to the extent that non-environmental capital and technology could not replace them. Natural and social sciences can only partially illuminate the trade-offs involved in these decisions; ultimately, they can only be made through an enlightened political process.

Turkey's economic development, most of which is concentrated in the coastal areas, continues to accelerate. One of the greatest challenges for the country's policy makers and managers will be to guide the development of Turkey's coastal areas in a sustainable way over the crucial decade of the 1990s. Should this opportunity be neglected, the loss to the environment - and to the economy - is likely to be very heavy and some of it irreversible.

An assessment of the coastal policies of OECD Member countries suggests that integrated management should be the basic approach to sustainable development of Turkey's coastal areas. Integrated management, however, requires an appropriate legal and administrative framework, rational planning, and special standards to protect highly fragile environments. This evaluation of Turkey's coastal policies, which builds on the collective experience of other OECD Member countries, is intended to offer guidance for future policies towards the sustainable development of coastal resources.

I. THE STATE OF COASTAL ZONES

1. *Main coastal features*

The Turkish coastal zone runs from the former Soviet border (presently Georgia) in the northeast, along the shores of the Black Sea, through the Straits of the Bosphorus and the Dardanelles, along the Sea of Marmara and, finally, along the coast of the Aegean and the Mediterranean in the west and south. With a total length of 8 272 kilometers, Turkey possesses one of the longest coast lines in OECD Europe. The climate is mild, particularly along the southern Mediterranean coast, and offers year-round tourism. Compared with the interior, with its much harsher climate, Turkey's coastal areas are also more attractive for urbanisation. (Figure 12)

Figure 12. **COASTAL PROVINCES**

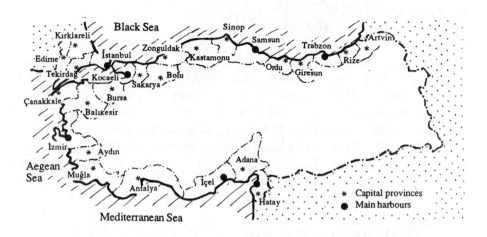

Turkey is framed by major, scenic coastal ranges along both the Black Sea and the Mediterranean. With two major exceptions, the country's rivers traverse the coastal zone and drain into Turkish coastal waters. Many bays and estuaries offer harbour facilities; some of these have been used since ancient times and others are currently under development to become marinas or oil facilities. Large tracts of the coastal ranges are heavily wooded and contain national parks of archaeological (Beydaglari), ornithological (Kus Cenneti) and ecological (Dilek Peninsula) importance.

The Turkish Coast Law of 1990 defines the coastal shore in terms of unrestricted public access and a construction setback margin. According to the law, **the shore** is delineated as the "foreshore between the low water mark and the highest water level, including estuaries, tidal rivers, and harbours". The **"shore strip"** is defined as a strip of dry land measuring up to 100 metres in depth. From a management point of view, it is now widely accepted that this definition of the coastal zone should be broadened to include coastal territorial waters, major river basins which affect these waters, or the coastal hinterland. In this chapter, the use of the term "coastal zone" refers to this broader territorial concept.

117

2.   *Urban and economic developments*

Coastal provinces as designated for administrative purposes cover 226 843 square kilometers or 29.2 per cent of Turkey's total area. According to the 1985 census, however, 47.5 per cent of the country's population resides in the coastal provinces. At present, due to the rapid drift of population towards the coast, this proportion exceeds 50 per cent. In 1985, Turkey's average population density was 65 persons per square kilometer as compared to about 130 in the coastal provinces. More importantly, Turkey's national population growth from 1980 to 1985 was 12.0 per cent as compared with 20.7 per cent in the coastal regions. Similarly, urban areas along the coast grew even faster, at 39.1 per cent compared with 27.5 per cent in all other urban areas (these are high growth rates by OECD standards). The consequences of these trends are reflected in unplanned housing developments, a lack of infrastructure, and the deterioration of urban and natural coastal areas and waters. (Figure 13)

The urban areas of the coast are important commercial and administrative centres; they are also the site of major concentrations of industrial, tourist, shipping and transport activity. In terms of population, the main coastal agglomerations are: Istanbul (6 million), Izmir (almost 2.5 million), Adana (approximately 2 million), Samsun, Icel and Hatay (approximately 1 million each), and Kocaeli and Antalya (over half a million each). (Figure 13)

The main industrial provinces are Istanbul, Izmir, Izmit, Adana, Mersin, Iskenderum and, to a lesser extent, two of the Black Sea provinces. The industries located in these areas are economically important, but highly polluting. They include: tanneries, textile and food processing plants, metal manufacturing, copper smelters, petroleum refineries, paint, artificial fertilizers, paper and pulp, and plastic manufacturing. Coal and copper mining is also part of the economic livelihood of the northern coastal region. Rough estimates suggest that between 70 and 80 per cent of all industrial output is produced in the coastal provinces. The severe environmental impact of such concentrations of industrial activity is reflected in the air and water quality measurements available for certain cities and bay areas. (Table 11)

Agricultural production, also a major economic activity in the coastal provinces, includes all types of products from industrial crops to cereals, fruits, and vegetables. It is worth noting that 90 per cent of total tobacco and sunflower seed production, 80 per cent of total cotton and corn production, and 70 per cent of total rice production, come from these provinces. The agricultural sector is under pressure from two contradictory trends: growing demand for food products (both for domestic consumption and for export) and the shrinking availability of

Figure 13. URBAN POPULATION IN COASTAL PROVINCES, 1985

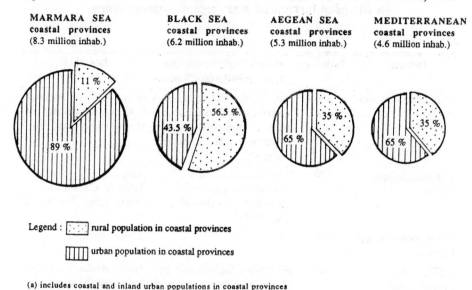

MARMARA SEA
coastal provinces
(8.3 million inhab.)

BLACK SEA
coastal provinces
(6.2 million inhab.)

AEGEAN SEA
coastal provinces
(5.3 million inhab.)

MEDITERRANEAN
coastal provinces
(4.6 million inhab.)

Legend : [::::] rural population in coastal provinces

[|||||] urban population in coastal provinces

(a) includes coastal and inland urban populations in coastal provinces

Source : adapted from : Ministry of Environment of the Republic of Turkey. *Turkish Background Report on Selected Environmental Topics* (1992).

fertile, rain-fed agricultural areas in the coastal provinces, where land is being diverted to urban and industrial uses. There is also pressure to reduce the agricultural pollution which has resulted from the intensive use of fertilizers and pesticides, to protect watersheds, and to manage land in a more sustainable manner.

Tourism is Turkey's "growth industry" and its largest single foreign exchange earner ($2.9 billion in 1990). In 1990, an estimated five million foreign tourists visited Turkey; the majority of them either visited or stayed on the coast. Over the last decade, foreign tourist arrivals increased at an exponential rate of over 40 per cent per year from about 0.9 million in 1982. The addition of domestic tourists, including those staying with relatives or in secondary housing, would double the figure to about 10 million tourists on the coast in 1990. Tourist bed capacity has increased by roughly 90 per cent during the last decade (from 200 000 beds in 1983 to 340 000 in 1989) and continues to expand. (Figures 14 and 15)

Both the public and the private sectors have made substantial investments in tourist facilities. Investment, which has been concentrated in expanding accommodation, increased from 11 billion TL in 1980 to 36 billion TL in 1989.

Table 11. **MAJOR INDUSTRIES AND THEIR TYPES OF WASTE in the Mediterranean and Aegean coastal zones**

Industry	Number	Probable pollutants and characteristics of effluents	Location
Food beverages and tobacco	250	Increase in BOD, suspended material, precipitable solid material, fat and oil Waste from tobacco and its treatment	Adana, Antalya, Aydin, Balikesir, Canakkale, Mugla, Hatay, Icel, Izmir
Textiles, clothing, leather	170	High amount of solid material, hardness, salt, sulphite, Cr, precipitable lime, BOD	Adana, Antalya, Aydin, Balikesir, Canakkale, Mugla, Hatay, Icel, Izmir
Wood products and furniture	15		Adana, Antalya, Balikesir, Icel, Izmir
Paper, paper products and printing industries	32	pH change, high amount of suspended solids, colloidal and dissolved material, paper supported material, cellulose	Adana, Aydin, Balikesir, Icel, Izmir, Mugla
Chemical, petroleum, coal, rubber and plastic products	62	pH change, organic and inorganic material, BOD, phenols, cyanides, nitrates, sulphites and phosphates SiO_2, $CaCO_3$, Al_2O_3, cobalt, cadmium, lithium in coal ash	Adana, Antalya, Aydin, Balikesir, Canakkale, Hatay, Icel, Izmir, Mugla
Non-metallic mineral products	59		Adana, Antalya, Aydin, Balikesir, Canakkale, Mugla, Hatay, Icel, Izmir
Metal goods, machinery, equipment, vehicles, scientific and professional measurement inst.	195		Adana, Antalya, Aydin, Balikesir, Hatay, Icel, Izmir, Mugla

Source: Ministry of Environment of the Republic of Turkey. *Turkish Background Report on Selected Environmental Topics* (1992).

Figure 14. ARRIVAL OF FOREIGN TOURISTS, 1965-1990

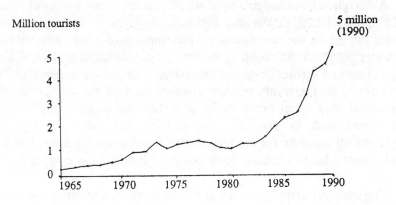

Source : State Institute of Statistics. *Statistical Indicators 1923-1990* (1991)

Figure 15. BALANCE OF FOREIGN TOURISM, 1965-1990

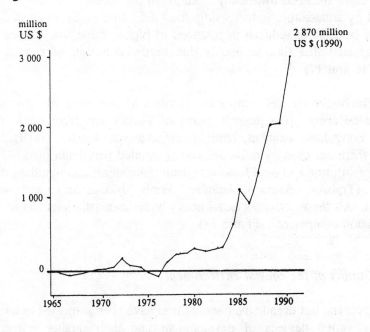

Source : State Institute of Statistics. *Statistical Indicators 1923-1990* (1991)

Investment incentives have included exemption from local taxes, concessional land allocation and cheap credit.

Although tourism has produced significant economic benefits in terms of gross foreign exchange inflow and regional employment, it has also made a substantial impact on the environment. The impacts of tourist activity include air and water pollution, reduction of the amount of unspoiled landscape, and the alteration of natural surroundings and the character of coastal settlements. These impacts have to be taken into account when evaluating the overall benefits of tourism which may often prove to be less than the gross foreign exchange inflows would tend to suggest. As tourism, industrial and agricultural developments all compete for the same natural and environmental resources - especially coastal land - conflicts have become more and more apparent.

Commercial fishing is another traditional economic activity which depends on uncontaminated coastal waters and non-interference from activities such as boating, sport fishing and sea transport. The lengthy Turkish coast, which is home to an estimated 363 fish species, provides good natural conditions for fishing and aquaculture. Total fishery production, more than 80 per cent of whose output comes from the Black Sea, reached almost 581 000 tonnes of fish in 1988, an increase of 48 per cent over 1980. In 1989, however, the quantity of fish caught declined drastically. Although the quantity of fish caught and produced by aquaculture is increasing, the total value of the catch is declining over time because of reduced populations of higher-value fish species. It has been suggested that this decline is due to the pollution of coastal waters. (Figures 16 and 17)

Harbours are very important features of the economic dynamism of some coastal areas. The main harbours of Turkey are, from north to south, Samsun, Zonguldak, Istanbul, Izmit, Izmir, Antalya, Mersin, and Iskenderun. Some of them are used by refineries and associated petroleum plants (Istanbul, Izmir, Mersin), iron and steel factories (Izmir, Iskenderum, Zonguldak), fertilizer factories (Trabzon, Samsun, Istanbul, Izmir, Iskenderun), and shipyards (Istanbul). All these activities entail heavy harbour installations and necessitate anti-pollution equipment. (Figure 18)

3.   *Quality of the coastal environment*

Over the last decade the coastal areas have been subjected to intense but regionally varied degrees of development and their quality reflects these pressures. Several areas appear to be badly polluted; others have been made

Figure 16. FISH CATCHES IN TURKISH MARINE WATERS, 1967-1989

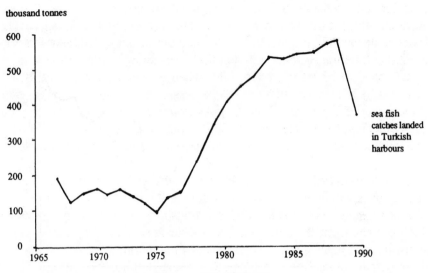

thousand tonnes

sea fish
catches landed
in Turkish
harbours

Source : State Institute of Statistics. *Statistical Indicators 1923-1990* (1991)

Figure 17. SEA FISH CATCHES by coastal region, 1989

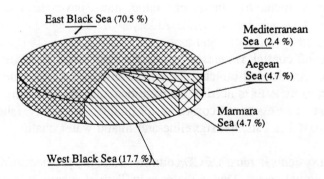

East Black Sea (70.5 %)

Mediterranean
Sea (2.4 %)

Aegean
Sea (4.7 %)

Marmara
Sea (4.7 %)

West Black Sea (17.7 %)

Source : Ministry of Environment of the Republic of Turkey. *Turkish Background Report on Selected Environmental Topics* (1992).

123

Figure 18. SEA TRANSPORTATION OF GOODS IN THE MAIN HARBOURS OF TURKEY, 1965-1990

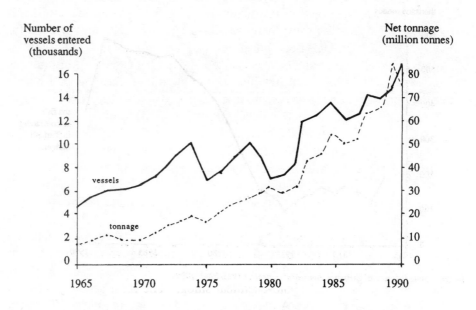

Source : State Institute of Statistics. *Statistical Indicators 1923-1990* (1991)

artificial. Still others, including some very large areas, have retained their pristine quality.

The variety of coastal resources, economic and urban activities has created a range of environmental effects. To obtain an adequate assessment of coastal quality, all of these effects need to be examined, and the following areas must be included in this assessment: coastal water quality, air quality, land and marine resources, coastal forests, the shoreline and inland water quality.

Information systems in most OECD countries can only provide sufficient data on a partial, regional basis. This is the case in Turkey, where information actually monitored, measured or calculated is fragmented and regionally specific. Under the circumstances, any assessment of the state of the environment in the coastal areas will be incomplete. More information is needed to assess the current situation and, even more importantly, to formulate and implement future policy effectively.

Land resources are under pressure from rapid urbanisation, industrialisation, tourism and infrastructure construction. As agricultural lands are being diverted to other uses, there is a decline in the availability of land for agricultural production and green areas. No precise information on the loss of agricultural land and other green areas is available, but the case of Izmir provides an indication of the trend: built-up areas of the metropolitan municipality have doubled within the last ten years, increasing from around 40 000 hectares to 80 000. This excludes the major developments around the metropolitan area: Kemalpasa, Cumaovasi, Torbali, Menemen, and Aliaga. Various construction projects have also triggered landslides and soil erosion. The widespread practice of removing sand and gravel from the shoreline has exacerbated this problem. In addition, wastes produced by industrial construction activity are being dumped along the shoreline and have led to soil degradation and water pollution.

Air pollution generated by private and commercial vehicles and by industrial, household and commercial heating is a major environmental problem in most of the urbanised coastal regions. In some cases this is exacerbated by atmospheric inversions and photo-chemical smog. The most severely affected areas are Istanbul, Izmit, Izmir, Antalya, Mersin, Adana, Iskerendun and Trabzon. Even small, non-industrial tourist areas, such as Bodrum, suffer from air pollution.

Coastal waters in many regions, especially bays and estuaries, are heavily polluted by any international standard. All of the coastal cities, as well as many other communities connected by rivers to the coast, discharge untreated household waste water into coastal waters. There are no deep sea outlets and, in many areas, the waters are too polluted for use of any kind. Industrial waste water is only minimally treated.

Almost 350 tonnes of BOD load, close to 1 200 g. of Hg, and a similar quantity of cadmium, are discharged daily into the Sea of Marmara. With the exception of certain limited regions, such as the northern entrance of the Bosphorus, only scant information is available on seawater concentration of pollutants. An examination of the effects of eutrophication in some parts of the Black Sea indicates that "conditions in the environment became lethal to the majority of organisms". (Figure 19)

Figure 19. BOD LOAD FROM COASTAL COMMUNITIES

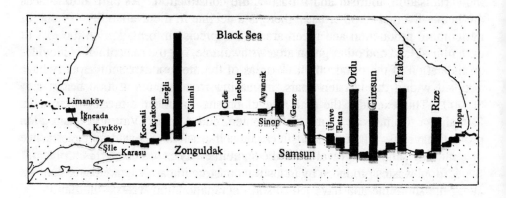

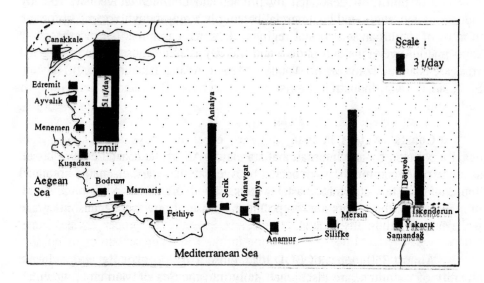

Source : Ministry of Environment of the Republic of Turkey, *Turkish Background Report on Selected Environmental Topics* (1992)

126

Many of the coastal areas serve as sites for important installations, such as ports, docking facilities, yachting harbors, and fishery installations. From 1984 to 1985, most of the major ports were equipped with port reception facilities for ballast water and tank washing. The southern Mediterranean coast usually receives heavy tanker traffic, an activity which creates oil pollution near the shoreline.

Turkey has a mixed economy, with substantial governmental involvement in all aspects of the economy. To cite just a few examples: governmental planning for economic development, government ownership in the industry and transport sectors, and state planning of tourism. Economic development in coastal areas is, therefore, only partially led by the market forces of the private sector. Responding to the comparative advantages of the coast, the government has been the driving force behind the development of these areas. Most central governmental departments, together with local governments, are already heavily involved in the management of the coast. Their operations and co-ordination are the crucial elements in shaping the economic and environmental future of these areas. In effect, government departments will determine whether these regions will develop in a sustainable manner. Because of its close involvement in coastal areas the government is in a relatively strong position to integrate environmental protection and coastal development and thereby ensure environmental integrity while pursuing its economic goals.

4.   *Environmental management*

From the perspective of environmental management there are two broad classes of governmental agencies: development agencies and "resource management and environmental agencies". The extent to which these development and environmental agencies are able to co-operate and integrate their various, often conflicting policies, is essential to proper coastal zone management. The Ministry of Interior through its representatives in coastal provinces, the governors, plays a vital role in balancing competing claims between "development agencies" and "resource management and environmental agencies".

The main development agencies

These include the Ministry of Industry and Trade, the Ministry of Tourism, the Ministry of Public Works and Settlement (including State Hydraulic

Works), the State Planning Organisation, the metropolitan municipalities and other major municipalities.

The **Ministry of Industry and Trade** and the **State Planning Organisation** (SPO) plan and implement industrial development. The SPO has both economic and financial responsibilities and is empowered to implement incentive schemes for regional development and to assist in indicative regional planning. Earlier industrial developments in the 1970s and 1980s triggered sudden migrations of the Turkish population to the country's coastal centres. Today, these population concentrations encourage further industrial development -- together with housing, commerce, large-scale infrastructure, etc. Although the objective of the SPO is to distribute economic development more or less evenly throughout the country, the policy has in fact led to a concentration of industrial activity, with all its environmental consequences, along the coast. Uncontrolled urbanisation and the proliferation of squatter settlements and illegal structures, most of which are without running water, sewerage systems or electricity, are the most striking manifestations of this trend. Although the SPO has a social department which considers environmental issues, it is not involved in environmental planning for the coast and its functions are limited to setting priorities for expenditure.

In recent years, the **Ministry of Tourism** (MOT) has become an important agent in coastal development. According to the Tourism Incentive Law of 1982, the Ministry has the mandate to develop and manage tourism areas located directly on the coast. The Ministry's activities are directed at the development of tourism facilities and attracting tourists. The MOT, which has increased powers now that tourism has been successfully extended along the Turkish coast, also has an influence over land ownership either through the transfer of government lands or by expropriation. The MOT also has the power and the resources to award leases to tourism developers on concessional terms and without Environmental Impact Assessments (EIAs).

The Ministry of Tourism has been highly successful in developing tourism, in attracting large numbers of tourists, and in expanding tourist facilities, particularly in terms of the number of beds. However, neither the MOT nor the SPO provides assessments of the net economic effects of tourism or of its cost and benefit to the environment. Most OECD Member countries now recognise the range and severity of the environmental effects of tourism, many of which are currently visible in Turkey. The MOT prepares master plans for designated tourist regions from which it plans Tourism Investment Areas at a scale of 1:1000, suitable for the implementation of individual sites. The chosen centres are, sometimes, preserved coastal natural areas; the beauty of their untouched landscape is thought to be the best reason for their touristic development. But the proposed facilities are generally to be built on the shore itself. This planning process, which is highly complex and involves 15 different agencies, covers only tourist centres.

Even in these areas, this planning process fails to assess the effects of pollution, the ratio of natural land to areas already built-up, and the protection of the shoreline. The process also appears to fail to recognise or address the problem of secondary housing, or the fact that development is destroying valuable tourist attractions such as the quality of the air and and the aesthetic value of the natural scenery.

In principle, tourist development outside tourist centres should also follow guidelines set by the MOT, receive supervision from the Ministry of Public Works and Settlement and be subject to approval by the local municipality or by the governor's office. In practice, however, there is little control or supervision in these areas.

The **Ministry of Public Works and Settlement** (MPWS), another powerful agency responsible for housing developments outside municipalities, grants permission for road and highway projects. Two of its departments, the State Hydraulic Works and the General Directorate of Bank of Provinces, are responsible for water supply and sewerage. Although driven by transport requirements, the ministry's road building programme also affects other developments along the coast. One such example is the construction of the highway along the southern Mediterranean coast. For most of its length, this highway runs along the ocean side of the mountains. Before the road existed most transport was conducted by sea. Indications are that future tourism development will take place along the new road, a trend which is likely to result in the disappearance of nature areas and other undesirable environmental effects. A proper EIA of the project would probably have recommended the construction of a highway along the inland side of the mountain range, leaving access roads to the coast in the valleys. This would have left the coastal areas largely intact.

Environment and resource management agencies

The **Ministry of Environment** (until recently the Undersecretariat for the Environment) bears the main responsibility for the "use and preservation of urban and rural land and of natural resources" in coastal regions, as well as for the prevention of water, soil and air pollution. The Ministry is also responsible for the "protection of plant and animal wealth and natural and historical riches", including marine resources. These functions, enshrined in the Environment Law of 1983 (enacted under the IVth Five-Year Development Plan), were embodied in specific objectives to be acted on during the course of the Vth Five-Year Development Plan (1985-1989). These objectives included: the elimination of existing pollution, the prevention of future pollution, and the preservation and development of resources for future generations. The recent VIth Five-Year Development Plan presents detailed environmental strategies to be implemented throughout the country, including all coastal regions.

In addition to this national legislation, Turkey has signed a number of international agreements and co-operation arrangements specifically designed to protect and manage the coastal land and water regions:

--   The Convention for the Protection of the Mediterranean Sea against Pollution and the Related Protocols;

--   MARPOL 73/78 Convention;

--   Intention to become a contracting party soon to the Convention on Wetlands of International Importance especially as Water Fowl Habitats;

--   Studies on Protection of the Black Sea against Pollution.

Hence, a number of laws, conventions and agreements are already in effect for the protection of the coastal areas and their adjoining waters.

The functions of the Ministry of Environment are described in Chapter 1 of this report. However, given the Ministry's overriding importance in coastal management, certain aspects of its operations merit a brief review. The effectiveness of the ministry has, until recently, been limited by a number of factors. For example, even at present, the Ministry has no permanent representatives based in Turkey's coastal regions and its provincial directorates, though established on paper, are not yet operational.

Enforcement of the 1990 Coast Law and related laws in the coastal regions is, in fact, carried out by the governors, who serve as the representatives of the central government in the provinces. Each governor's secretariat, within which the various governmental departments are represented, implements the law in the provinces. However, for various other purposes (for example, land use) the governor's responsibility is limited to territories outside the municipal limits. Nevertheless, it is the governor's responsibility to ensure that the municipalities implement the Environment Law. In principle, the governor's office, the Metropolitan Municipalities, and to a lesser degree the other municipalities, carry the major responsibility for implementing environmental policy. Their co-operation and willingness to implement these laws are decisive, particularly in matters of pollution control.

The **Specially Protected Areas** (SPAs) cover nine coastal zones, as well as three interior sites (see list). An Authority originally created under the Barcelona Convention to prevent marine pollution has been redefined as a development agency for the protection areas under its jurisdiction. The new Authority's powers include land use management as well as environmental management. The Agency will also take on duties and prerogatives of the Ministry of Environment, the Ministry of Tourism, the Ministry of Agriculture and Rural Affairs, the Ministry of Forestry, and the municipalities. This system of direct administration over part of the national territory in the coastal regions is a new and interesting development. The agency combines all the major responsibilities a coastal administrative system should ideally comprise: control of seashore urbanisation, in-depth planning for new inland urban centres, protection of historic sites, forests and agricultural zones; control over excessive coastal densities; pollution prevention of coastal waters; and the protection of drinking water catchment basins. The Authority for Specially Protected Areas (ASPA), however, is still in the planning stages. Based in Ankara, the ASPA cannot take over local responsibilities from other departments because it has a shortage of staff. Even though the ASPA should assume responsibility for integrated territorial development, its authority appears to be superseded by the State Planning Organisation in the area of financial co-ordination.

The **Ministry of Agriculture and Rural Affairs** is an important agency in terms of both implementing agricultural policy and managing agricultural land. Both of these responsibilities have important implications for coastal areas. Agricultural activities can lead to the pollution of coastal rivers, wetlands and coastal waters; management of land use in agricultural areas can affect the quality of urban, industrial and tourism development. Until recently, agricultural land in Turkey was protected against transfer to other uses, providing it was flat, arable land of high quality and particularly if it had been used for irrigation agriculture. The policy logic underlying this legislation was that rapid population growth would necessitate the production of relatively cheap food, particularly on those high quality coastal lands situated close to major development centres. However, this particular law was changed in 1989 in a manner which has permitted almost unrestricted transformation of agricultural land. Rainfed agricultural land can be diverted to urban, industrial and commercial uses, as well as to highway construction or tourist development. Irrigated land can be

TOURISM AND NATURE CONSERVATION: DALYAN

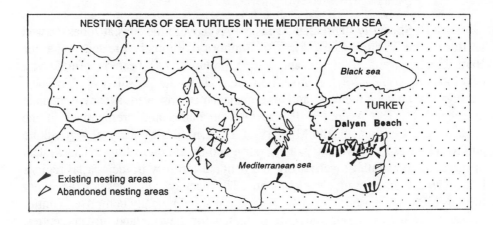

NESTING AREAS OF SEA TURTLES IN THE MEDITERRANEAN SEA

The sea turtles: endangered around the world

The sea turtle, a 95-million-year-old marine reptile, is now endangered and threatened with extinction worldwide; this concerns all species of it. Sea turtles nest in warm waters around the world, including in the Mediterranean. To lay their eggs, they return to the same beach where they themselves hatched. The eggs are laid at night 40-60 cm deep in the sand, and the incubation period is about 55 days. An average nest contains 90-100 eggs. Only one egg out of 1000 will reach maturity.

Among the numerous threats (marine pollution, sand and shingle extraction, swallowing of plastic bags instead of jelly-fish; the turtles may be accidentally caught by fishermen, hunted for food or for trade, or killed; other animals may prey on their nests, etc.), threats from tourism appear to be the most serious ones: apartment homes and hotels are built on beaches, cement is poured across the coastal sand close to the edge of the water; in the nesting period (June to August), speed boats kill or injure turtles at sea, vehicles crush eggs or leave deep tracks which may become threats for hatchlings, etc. All these factors are detrimental to the reproduction of the sea turtles because they prevent the mother turtles from crossing the beach, digging the sand and laying eggs; artificial lights disorient the hatchlings when they head towards the brighter sea at night, which means that they die from over-exposure when the sun rises the following day.

The Dalyan beach: a key Mediterranean reproduction site for sea turtles

In the western Mediterranean basin, sea turtles have disappeared in the last few decades. In the eastern Mediterranean basin, recent observations have shown that the turtle population is seriously declining. Several sea turtle nesting beaches exist in Turkey. In 1988, DHKD (Society for the Protection of Nature), a national NGO (non-governmental organisation), and WWF (World Wide Fund for Nature) identified along the Mediterranean coast, 17 sites where sea turtles still nest. These beaches host the largest known numbers, in the Mediterranean, of two species of sea turtles: the loggerhead turtle *Caretta caretta* and the more confined green turtle *Chelonya mydas*.

One of these sites is the Dalyan beach. Large numbers of loggerhead turtles nest at Dalyan, at the western edge of the nesting grounds of that species in Turkey. Together with the nearby beaches of Dalyanagzi (0.2 km) and Ekincik (0.4 km), the Dalyan beach (4.0 km) is part of a wider lagoon-type ecosystem (the Köycegiz lagoon) which had been remarkably preserved from human presence until a few years ago.

Conservation efforts in the face of tourism development pressures

Nonetheless, tourism development plans started to be drawn up for the entire coastline around the lagoon; a hotel complex was planned on the beach itself. Local and national Turkish associations for the protection of nature initiated protest actions and scientific studies in order to promote the protection of the whole area. They were supported by international nature conservation associations (WWF in particular). In the framework of the Barcelona Convention, a partial solution was found in 1988 by designating the Dalyan beach as a "specially protected area" (SPA). This SPA was enlarged in 1990.

Since 1988 ANPT has undertaken specific forms of action on the Dalyan beach in order to limit the impacts of human frequentation on the nesting activities of turtles at night: lines of wooden pickets have been set into the sand, clearly marking off the part of the beach which is frequented by the sea turtles and their hatchlings. But the respect of this limit is left to the appreciation of the tourists since the area does not have a reserve-type status.

Other problems have to be solved for a better conservation of the area:

- Because of the abandoned hotel foundation on the beach, the natural water inlet through the sandy cordon to the lagoon is becoming partially filled and the balance of flows between land, sea and lagoon is upset.
- Heavy motor boat traffic through the canal joining the sea to the lagoon destabilizes the currents regulating the inputs and outputs of this fragile ecosystem.
- In spite of a governmental decision which should have fostered conservation of the site and protection of the sea turtles, the local response to summer tourism demand has been to open the site to daily human frequentation and authorise the building of wooden cabins at the top of the beach, to meet the need for food distribution and for public toilets.
- In 1990, the ASPA (Ministry of Environment's Authority for Specially Protected Areas) prepared plans for the construction of several tourist facilities on the beach; wood panels were attached to iron fixtures sunk into concrete blocks, themselves deeply installed in the sand of the beach. Moreover, it is now planned to transform the abandoned concrete foundations of the hotel (about 100 sq.m) into a 250-car car-park instead of removing them from the beach.

What future for Dalyan beach?

It is not clear that the Dalyan site has been protected sufficiently and for a sufficient time: it is estimated that the rate of protection will be about 70 per cent. Protection will only be achieved:
- if the site receives a reserve status; and
- if tourism development concepts, locally and nationally, change so as to adopt the objective of sustainability, that is the sufficient protection of the very resource on which tourism is based: the quality of the natural and cultural environment.

transferred to co-operatives with 1000 members, or to export-oriented industries and commercial centres. Since 1000-member tourist co-operatives are easily formed in Turkey, there is nothing to prevent tourism or mass housing developments from invading coastal agricultural land. The protection of coastal agricultural land is clearly no longer effective.

The Ministry of Forestry manages the coastal wooded area designated under the Forestry Law. Wooded areas in Turkey peripheral to the central Anatolian Plain occupy 11 million hectares. The Turkish coastline, with its combination of sea, forest and mountains, is both a precious landscape and one of the country's major environmental and ecological assets. The Ministry of Forestry, until recently under the authority of the Ministry of Agriculture and Rural Affairs, is now an independent administrative body. According to the 1937 Forestry Law, the entire Turkish forest is inalienable government property. While the law recognises the forest's recreational and aesthetic value, its economic use is deemed paramount. Forests in the coastal areas fulfill a variety of crucial environmental functions. They serve as part of the hydrological system, absorb greenhouse gases, provide protection against landslides and create a habitat for fauna and flora. Within the forest areas, national parks have been established and placed under the special protection of the National Park Department of Ministry of Forestry (those on the coast include Beydaglari, Termessos, Dilek Peninsula and Gelibolu Peninsula). Despite the existence of laws protecting forests and national parks, the Ministry of Tourism is empowered to designate "tourist regions", which thereby supersede all other protective measures. This trend has already occurred in various regions of the coast; as a result, woodland areas are shrinking.

The Ministry of Culture has been given the authority, through the Law on Protection of Natural and Cultural Resources, to protect certain historic and archaeological sites. Many of these sites are situated in coastal areas, particularly on the west and southwest coasts from Troy to Ephesus, Helicarnassus, Side, and Antioch. As part of its management of these areas, the Ministry prepares and executes protective plans which are presumed to supersede any previously existing legislation. However, building permits can still be issued within the protected areas and are subordinate to other laws. In some cases, protected lands have been designated for tourist uses. On the whole, very few areas (with the exception of Phaselis, for example) are actually managed as historical sites.

II. EVALUATION OF COASTAL ZONE MANAGEMENT

As a general observation, the examination of the coastal areas shows that a significant area of the Turkish coast is still either in its natural state or only minimally affected by development. The reasons for this are threefold: the Turkish coastline is very extensive and there is room for development; secondly, modern coastal development in Turkey is very recent, particularly in the field of tourism and industry; thirdly, attempts to manage the coast date back to the 1960s and 1970s.

From an environmental perspective, coastal zone management needs to be evaluated according to the following criteria:

-- Integration of policy objectives and achievements;

-- Administrative structures for implementing policy;

-- Availability of legal instruments;

-- Financial mechanisms to achieve objectives;

-- Implementation of environmental policy in coastal areas.

1. *Integration of policy objectives and achievements*

During the past decade, the two main policy objectives for the development of the coastal areas have been industrialisation and tourism. These were partly accompanied and partly led by urbanisation and infrastructure development, particularly in the field of transport. It is understandable that a country like Turkey, with its high population growth and low per capita income relative to other OECD Member countries, should give economic objectives relatively high priority.

From the environmental perspective, two related and unfavourable factors - the speed of development and the unco-ordinated nature of policies - have resulted in the partial degradation of Turkey's coastal resources. No OECD Member country in recent history has developed coastal areas at the speed at which this is occurring today in Turkey. Nor is it conceivable that Turkey, or any country undertaking such rapid development, would not encounter major conflicts between its economic requirements, its environmental policies, and its development goals.

The contradictions between industrialisation and tourism are becoming more and more visible; short-term effects are already evident, for example, in the Antalya and Izmir regions. If Turkey fails to re-evaluate policy objectives over the medium- and long-term, policymakers will be deprived of certain options. A similar conflict occurs between agricultural and other economic development objectives: good arable land is now being diverted to non-agricultural uses, while in other areas, lower quality land is being developed to the detriment of overall agricultural production.

As regards the integration of environmental objectives with plans for the economic development of the coastal provinces, there is very little evidence of any progress. In spite of major planning efforts, the underlying economic and environmental policy which defines these objectives remains unco-ordinated.

2. *Administrative arrangements for coastal management*

As has been shown earlier, practically all governmental agencies are present in coastal areas and participate in their development. The metropolitan and other municipalities also have a major role to play in land use planning.

Like many other OECD Member countries, Turkey has suffered from overlaps and gaps in its administration. In some cases there are too many agencies, while in others there are too few. Management by the central government can be too distant, but municipal administration can be too close and controlling. The most serious administrative problem, however, is the absence of an overall environmental management scheme in the coastal regions. Finally, there is no clear administrative consensus or understanding of the basic objectives and territorial limits of coastal management.

Confused land-use management and the associated, unplanned industrial, commercial and tourist facilities are the result of gaps and overlaps in the allocation of responsibilities to the various levels of government. Illegal settlements continue to multiply and municipalities are partly unable, partly unwilling, to intervene. Unless this process is controlled to allow both municipal planning and infrastructure construction to catch up with urban growth, this chaotic situation will continue. There is no evidence that the Turkish authorities have made great progress in their efforts to control illegal settlements.

Similar gaps or overlaps are appearing between tourist and industrial planning, a situation which has resulted in parallel development in the same area. This is particularly true in territories which fall outside the municipal boundaries.

136

The governor's office, which is theoretically responsible for the management of these areas, has in fact failed to assert its authority in many coastal regions.

There is, in fact, no environmental management on the part of the central government in the coastal regions. The Ministry of Environment has no offices in the provinces, with the exception of an occasional visit from the central office in Ankara. The representative of the Ministry of Health is part of the governor's office, but his responsibilities are defined by the Health Law and relate mainly to the quality of drinking water. The other departmental representatives are more concerned with development and generally tend to subordinate environmental considerations to their main objectives. The municipalities, which have attempted to apply environmental regulations, find themselves handicapped in enforcing charges, penalties and closures because many offending plants are government-owned.

The administrative framework lacks the cohesion and legal power to define the boundaries of the appropriate territory for coastal management. Although the coastal provinces under the authority of the governor would come close to the idea of an administrative entity for coastal management, most agencies do not recognise them as such. In many cases, these provinces lack sufficient depth in the hinterland or width along the coast. As a result, the rivers and land in the river basin areas have not been managed with their potential impact on the coast in mind. The impact of developments in the hinterland on the coast and in coastal waters takes the form of pollution, high population density and the disappearance of green areas. Similarly, the unco-ordinated nature of planning between coastal provinces is reflected in unbroken shoreline development.

3.   *Availability of legal instruments for coastal management*

As the list of agencies indicates, practically all government departments and all levels of government are heavily involved in coastal management. Consequently, all the laws and regulations governing these agencies are applicable in these areas. As recently as April 1990, the Turkish government passed a coastal law and issued an application decree pertaining to the "definition, use and planning" under the law.

The various pieces of legislation have developed over time in an *ad hoc* manner, with no overall policy framework. As a result, there are considerable contradictions between the various laws and no clear understanding as to which should prevail. Current practice indicates that the most recent legislation is given preference; the development of "tourist regions", for example, takes precedence over the preservation of agricultural or forest land.

Furthermore, the "Coast Law" has not proved to be highly effective in protecting the coast. The law provides definitions of the coastal space, procedures for its use, and limits for its physical modification. Here again, to implement this law would require a high degree of co-operation between a number of ministries. Nevertheless, the Coast Law is the only law which transcends all powers, whether Ministerial, provincial or local, requiring a setback margin. This margin is, however, fixed at a maximum of 100 metres, beyond which anything is possible. Furthermore, the manner in which the law is to be implemented remains unclear, especially the extent to which structures built prior to its enactment can be demolished or modified.

4. *Financial arrangements for the various policy objectives*

As a general proposition, it is true to say that environmental protection in Turkey is under-financed relative to the needs for protection. This is particularly true for the protection of coastal zones where the environmental effects of development are severe. In contrast, the subsidising of developmental activities can, in some cases, amount to the subsidising of pollution.

Turkish industry is currently subsidised through preferential local tax treatment, allocation of land and - as is the case with some government factories - through direct subsidies. Similarly, tourism is given preferential treatment through the allocation of municipal land, exemption from local taxes and preferential interest loans.

In contrast there is little finance available for the construction of municipal waste water treatment plants or for pollution control facilities in government-owned enterprises. The only special financing facility pertains to the purchase of garbage collection trucks for municipalities.

This contradictory financing policy augurs badly for future environmental policy implementation. Unless sufficient finance is made available or generated from local sources it will be impossible to protect coastal areas from the effects of the extensive development now underway.

138

5. *Implementation of environmental policy in coastal areas*

For the reasons cited above - contradictory policy objectives and legislation, weak administrative integration, lack of relevant legislation, and environmentally harmful financing arrangements - environmental policy is implemented in a haphazard and limited manner. Pollution control regulations for industrial enterprises are not rigorously enforced and fines have proven to be ineffectual. Weak protection of natural areas outside the specially protected zones and the absence of municipal waste water treatment and industrial pollution controls have resulted in severely polluted waters off many areas of the coast.

In general, a coherent environmental policy is absent: the implementation of existing regulation is either weak or non-existent, environmental impact assessments are rare, and there is only nascent recognition of the need to prevent environmental degradation.

The results of this evaluation of the major causes of environmental degradation of Turkey's coastal areas, including coastal waters and marine resources, provide a framework of recommendations for improved management. The assessment of the quality of the coastal areas indicates that although many areas of the coast are still untouched, the rate of deterioration in some areas, the rapid spread of pollution, and other effects all require immediate corrective action. Unless some action is taken in the very near future, damage to coastal resources - including economic damage - will accelerate and could, for example, result in the total and irreversible collapse of bay areas and the extinction of fish species in some coastal regions.

Authorities need to recognise and seize opportunities for action which require minimum additional finance and whose effects will be immediate and long lasting. This needs to begin with a concerted effort to integrate policy formulation and implementation.

There are therefore five broad areas for policy recommendation:

-- **Reconciliation** of policy objectives in coastal regions with special regard for sustainable development of coastal resources;

-- **Integration** of the administrative arrangements for coastal management and appropriate definition of areas from both the regional and the national point of view;

-- **Creation** of a legal framework through the drafting of a new coastal law and with the reconciliation of existing laws;

-- **Vigorous implementation** of existing environmental laws and regulations through co-operation between municipalities and the Governors of the coastal provinces.

-- **Creation of financing mechanisms** for coastal protection through a combination of central government funds and regional funds generated by local taxes, fines, penalties, user charges and tourism development fees; the discontinuation of subsidies for polluting activities.

III. CONCLUSIONS AND RECOMMENDATIONS

1. *Policy formulation*

As coastal areas are some of Turkey's most valuable natural resources, their management should be given high priority at the Cabinet level. Policy objectives for coastal areas must be clearly defined at the highest political level in order to minimise and eliminate potential conflicts. In the case of coastal areas, these policy issues include:

Population growth in coastal areas: the government needs to define the rate of population growth at which it can provide housing and supply adequate infrastructure. The current lack of a policy has led to the proliferation of illegal settlements, which need to be reduced to manageable proportions. Corresponding measures to control tourist and industrial developments are outlined below.

The role of tourism in coastal areas: to be compatible with sustainable coastal developments, the rate of tourism industry growth must take into account future population growth in these regions; industrial development must be compatible with tourism development and the need for coastal conservation.

A balanced regional development policy: developments along the coast and between coastal and hinterland regions need to be balanced to reduce the pressure on coastal areas; also, coastal development should correspond to the natural advantages and carrying capacities of both the individual region and its adjoining coastal areas. Coastal zone issues should be discussed by ministers in the Environment/Natural Resource Cabinet Committee or in other economic development Cabinet Committees of which the Minister of Environment is an automatic member as already proposed in Chapter 2 with a view to:

-- **Defining the above objectives in quantitative terms** for the medium and long term;

-- **Eliminating or minimising policy conflicts** between the various coastal zones and other development goals;

-- **Ensuring that sustainable development** as a guiding principle will be given due political recognition.

The Environment/Natural Resource Cabinet Committee should include the Ministers of Finance, Public Works and Settlement, Agriculture and Rural Affairs, Industry and Trade, Tourism and the Environment and should review both developments and policy objectives for coastal areas on a routine basis.

2. *Coastal zone legislation*

At present the new Coast Law (1990) and a number of other laws relate directly or indirectly to coastal management. Two steps are needed to strengthen existing legislation: a review and revision of the Coast Law of 1990; the reconciliation of various existing legislations.

The Coast Law should be reviewed for the effectiveness of both the "set-back limits" for construction and the "boundaries of the zones" for management purposes. The various limits defined for "set-back" from the highest water level (shore border line) should be extended to ensure effective protection of shore areas. Although construction on the "shore strip" is prohibited, no guidance is given for the proper maintenance of the strip. Activities harmful to the shore, such as dumping and mining, should be prohibited by law. At present, the Coastal Law gives a definition of the boundaries of the coastal zone. However, these boundaries appear to be drawn too narrowly for effective management. A revision of the law needs to extend these boundaries along the lines described below.

The overlap and contradictions in **existing laws** need to be reviewed, reconciled and/or eliminated. More specifically, the Tourism Law appears to be interpreted at present to override other land uses (for example, agriculture) and conservation priorities. The Settlement Development Act, which prescribes planning regulations for all kinds of construction, also appears to override environmental concerns. A revision of these laws needs to begin with the elimination of obvious contradictions and then move to minimise those "grey areas" left to the discretion of the governor or to the various departments and

141

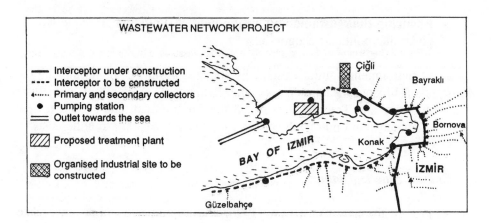

WASTEWATER NETWORK PROJECT

— Interceptor under construction
--- Interceptor to be constructed
◄····· Primary and secondary collectors
● Pumping station
═ Outlet towards the sea

▨ Proposed treatment plant

▧ Organised industrial site to be constructed

The İzmir bay: fast-growing pressures

On the Aegean sea, the Metropolitan Municipality of İzmir area (1.75 million inhabitants in 1990) includes the city of İzmir located at the eastern part of the İzmir bay, and 10 other municipalities around the central part of the bay. The growth of the city started to accelerate in the mid 1960s, due to migration from rural areas. Higher population growth rates are forecasted for the years to come with 4.85 million inhabitants in an extended metropolitan İzmir for the year 2020.

İzmir has the second biggest port and is the third largest city in Turkey, and is an important industrial and commercial regional centre. Today there are 6 000 industrial establishments in İzmir, against 1 353 in 1986. Most of them are located in the inner bay, although in recent years industrial developments have tended to move outwards. Three groups of industries include a high number of factories, each producing highly polluting wastes:

- leather industry: 94 tanneries producing (at least) 30 000 hides/year and 40 000 tonnes leather/year are discharging wastes directly into the inner bay: for example, the phenolic compounds load is 1 900 kg/year (1985). The recorded figures are high and the actual figures are likely to be higher since many establishments are not registered;

- paint-producing industry: 14 plants produce about 155 000 tonnes paint/year; waste waters have a high chemical oxygen demand, high solid and heavy metal loads and contain several toxic organic substances. Pollutants in these waste waters cannot be removed by conventional treatment techniques nor by use of secondary treatment methods;

- textile industry: five main factories are registered in İzmir; but numerous small factories also discharge organic pollution equivalent to that from a population of 10 000.

Resulting from these growing demographic and economic pressures, the environmental degradation of the bay has made it one of the most polluted areas in Turkey. Monitoring shows that the inner bay is heavily polluted and eutrophication has started: the main sources of pollution appear to be the streams flowing into the bay and carrying domestic and industrial wastes.

Reducing pollution in the bay of İzmir

Despite early concern, attempts and plans, the urban area today lacks a sewerage and storm drainage system. Funding to build a lagoon-type wastewater treatment plant, interceptors, pump stations and major collectors and trunks was approved by the World Bank in 1985; final design of the network was approved in 1988 and implementation started. With the completion of this programme most organic wastes from industrial and urban origins around the Bay will be collected and treated before being discharged into the bay waters. Also, in 1988, the Metropolitan Municipality of İzmir began a three-year environmental baseline monitoring programme for the bay as an international co-operation programme involving the State Planning Office, the World Bank and the UNEP/MAP/PAP (Priority Actions Programme of the Mediterranean Action Plan of UNEP), and co-ordinated by the former Ministry of Environment.

Relocation and grouping of industries is also considered. For example, a new industrial area is to be established in the northwestern part of the bay; it would be about 3.5 km long, and 1.7 km wide. A large variety of industrial activities will be established in this area where about 500 factories are expected to be built, generating an organic pollution equivalent to that from a population of 50 000 persons. These effluents will be treated by a separate wastewater treatment plant. However, heavy metal pollution will have to be prevented in another way.

The wastewater management project should contribute to the improvement of the water quality of the bay. The completion of the network for wastewater treatment will not, however, fully protect the bay from environmental degradation. An integrated management and decision-making framework concerning the use of the natural resources of the Bay is needed. There is an opportunity for co-operation between central and local authorities through the joint UNEP/MAP/PAP and Metropolitan Municipality of İzmir planning study. Strengthening the involvement of regional authorities would also ensure a more efficient implementation of projects. Political commitment to improvement of the bay environment, already clear concerning the wastewater management project, is essential to support future funding. Staff training, public involvement for a bay-wide planning approach, the use of clear environmental impact assessment procedures, and the generation of basic information on the physical, biological and social conditions of the bay are other basic elements needed for the integrated management of the bay area and its surroundings. Decision-enforcement will require a combination of legal, institutional and economic instruments.

which could potentially damage the environment. This review recommends that all overriding powers be abolished and that government agencies acting as developers should be subject to the same rules as private enterprise. The revisions need to ensure that the law is interpreted according to the priorities of sustainable management. It is also recommended that special attention be given to providing better safeguards for areas of high conservation value so that these can be protected more securely than at present.

3. *Institutional framework for integrated management*

Many of the problems of the coastal zone are the same as those of other areas and the institutional arrangements established in those areas should in principle be the starting point for those applying in the coastal zone. What is different in the coastal zone, however, is the intense pressure of competing demands all appearing to converge on relatively small areas. It is this concentration of issues all needing to be taken into account at the same time that requires some special provision to ensure the integration of decision-making. Chapter 2 presented three possible options for integrated environmental management and the special Coastal Zone Management Councils proposed here would fit in with whatever option is finally selected by the Turkish government.Membership of the Coastal Zone Management Councils - which could vary from region to region - should be decided according to the functions of the management units. Since the objective is integrated management, it is essential that all the major decision-makers participate. These councils should include: the provincial government represented by the local municipalities, the governor, the major development ministries (Public Works and Settlement, Tourism, Agriculture and Rural Affairs, Industry and Trade, State Planning Organisation), the environment and conservation ministries (Environment, Culture, Forestry) and, where appropriate, the Regional Environment Agency. These management authorities would require a small permanent staff and basic financial resources. Since provincial environmental directorates are likely to be established, these units can serve as a secretariat and act as the lead agency.

Legislation establishing the Coastal Zone Management Councils should also precisely define the functions of these councils along the following lines:

-- **Responsibility** for convening meetings and serving as a lead agency;

-- **Responsibility** for compiling Coastal Resource Inventories which provide the information based on which future management decisions can be founded;

-- **Notification procedure** for development projects;

-- **Methods** for Environmental Impact Assessments (EIAs);

-- **Decision-making process**;

-- **Monitoring**.

The role of Coastal Zone Management Councils (CZMC) will be to ensure integrated management. Each major project (industrial, tourist, agricultural, infrastructural, landscape altering) will need to be assessed according to precise guidelines and examined by the CZMC in co-operation with all the development, resource management and environmental protection agencies. The CZMC will assess these proposals for mutual compatibility and long-term sustainability. The CZMCs' responsibility for examining and approving coastal projects within their management areas would override that of the individual departments, the governor and the municipalities.

4. *Implementation and financing*

Implementation and financing should be administered by the government and the municipalities, using all the provisions and mechanisms already in place in the various policy areas as well as whatever specific instruments of implementation are deemed necessary for the coastal zone.

Implementation should comprise the following components:

-- Long-term indicative plans by major coastal regions; detailed land-use plans for both the municipalities and areas outside their administration;

-- Plans for the development of coastal waters (marinas, aquaculture, and reclamation);

-- Overall development of the coastal areas according to directions of CZMC authorities;

-- Implementation of the Environment Law and Health Law both on coastal land and in coastal waters through the use of regulatory and economic instruments. These should include: specific actions to restore damaged ecosystems (such as estuaries and bays), critical habitats, and the living conditions of endangered species;

145

-- Special financing measures for the coastal regions;

-- Specific measures complying with international obligations in coastal zones, with particular attention to coastal waters.

Long-term plans by major coastal regions should be prepared in collaboration by the appropriate ministries, including the national environmental authorities. These plans should identify the areas where developments are likely to be concentrated over the next 20 to 25 years. Such indicative plans would assist local authorities in the preparation of land-use plans, and those responsible for environmental infrastructure, with particular attention to sewerage.

Land-use planning at the municipal level is a crucial element in defining both the population density and industrial activity along the coast and, therefore, the likely pressures on the environment. Consequently, land-use planning should be developed with environmental considerations in mind. These should include the pollution loads, the aesthetic (landscape) aspect and the provision of green areas. Present land-use planning practices need to be significantly upgraded and improved. In a context where land rights are often disputed, there is an urgent need for the clarification of ownership and for the establishment of a land register. In order to prevent coastal erosion, the removal of sand and shingle from the shoreline needs to be controlled on the basis of coastal resource inventories and an understanding of the longshore sediment transport processes along the particular stretch of coastline.

Overall development of coastal management areas should be directed by the relevant CZMC. Each project is to be judged according to an EIA statement, its compatibility with land-use planning, the carrying capacity of the environment, and the population capacity of the area. This process should comply with established regional norms and these criteria should be developed and applied to the entire range of land, air and water resources both on land and in coastal waters.

The CZMC, as defined by national legislation, should also take responsibility for the sustainable management of coastal water and marine resources.

Implementation of the Environment Law and the Health Law is crucial for successful coastal management. While this is of general concern to Turkey as a whole, it is a particularly urgent issue in the coastal areas. It is in the economic interest of these areas that coastal water quality correspond to bathing water quality, as defined by the Barcelona Convention and its protocols. In the case of water pollution control from land-based sources, three measures need to be urgently enforced:

-- Any new installation should be allowed to operate only when it is monitored and found to be in compliance with the appropriate pollution controls;

-- Old and highly polluting installations should be closed within a relatively short time unless they can be retrofitted and rendered profitable;

-- All municipalities and major tourist sites should have proper sewage treatment and disposal systems.

These measures need to be supplemented by controls governing sea-based activities:

-- Ocean dumping and the incineration of hazardous substances;

-- Marine pollution from shipping, including the discharge of ballast water;

-- Pollution from harbour activities.

Implementation of these measures needs to come through close co-operation between the Province Environment Directorates, the Regional Environment Agencies, the governor's office and the municipalities. In the short term, implementation will be circumscribed by the availability of financing. Over the medium and long term, however, integrated management is likely to bring substantial benefits to localities, even generating funds to finance the cost of pollution control. A study of Izmir Bay suggests that the economic benefits of cleaning the bay over a 35-year period will outweigh the cost by a factor of three or more.

The financing problem over the short run should be solved through a combination of financing mechanisms: central government funds, local taxes, charges for services, pollution taxes, and private financing. Due to the intense and rapid rate of development in coastal areas, the financing problem is particularly acute. At the same time, the capacity of the coastal regions to pay for certain services and charges is substantially greater than in other areas of the country. Moreover, the reduction of subsidies currently provided for tourism and industrial development in the coastal areas could both reduce the pressure on the environment and generate additional funds for infrastructure and protection.

POLLUTION CONTROL: THE ISKENDERUN GULF AREA

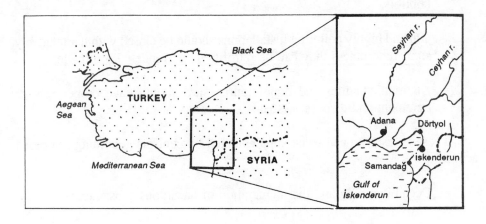

A variety of land-based pollutions

The Gulf of İskenderun has about 180 km of shores in the eastern part of the Mediterranean basin and is situated roughly between the Adana plain and the Syrian border. Two large cities are located near its shores: Adana (almost one million inhabitants) and Antakya (over one hundred thousand inhabitants). Both have industrial zones connected with other industrial centres and harbours (Karataş, Dörtyol, İskenderun, Yakacik, Samandag). The rivers flowing into the Gulf collect waters from the hinterlands where agricultural production of crops, such as cotton, is intensive and of major importance for Turkey. Two rivers, the Seyhan and the Ceyhan, form sandy deltas in the vicinity of Adana. They are still largely wild and preserved. East of them is Dörtyol harbour; since 1969, it has been the terminus of pipelines carrying Iraqi oil up to the Mediterranean coast. The continental shelf is wide and shallow. Because of the large input of fresh water and sediments from rivers, the Gulf offers considerable potential for fish and shrimp production.

In the absence of significant environmental investments and of effective implementation of environmental policies, the Gulf receives heavy pollution loads of:

- nutrients and pesticides from the fields of the Çukurova plain drained by the Ceyhan and Seyhan rivers;

- organic pollution from cities;

148

- organic, chemical and metallic (Hg, Pb, Cr, Zn, Cd) pollution produced by industries (textile, foodstuffs, paint, soda, paper, mines, etc.);

- tar coming from tankers, oil refineries and oil processing plants; excessive amounts of tar have been recorded in the Gulf waters, whereas the terminal facilities of the two pipelines transferring oil from Iraq do not seem to be themselves a major source of pollution.

An integrated management plan for the sustainable development of the area

The sustainable development of several key activities of the region depends upon maintaining the quality of the environment (air, water, marine) and the availability of natural resources such as fresh water and soil. Therefore an integrated management plan has been in preparation since 1990 for the İskenderun Gulf area; relating objectives of economic development and of environmental and natural resources preservation, it is known as the "İskenderun project" and was launched by the former Turkish Under-Secretariat for Environment. The preparation of the plan is technically, scientifically and financially supported by the UNEP-Mediterranean Action Plan and conducted by the Faculty of Political Sciences of Ankara University, under the supervision of the Ministry of Environment, in close co-operation with the local authorities. The project is to be completed by 1992.

The dynamic relationships between regional economic development scenarios and their likely impacts on the environment are being studied, as a tool to help choosing the main pollution-prevention measures. The model relies on a large data-collecting network and on socio-economic and environmental indicators. The environmental impacts of the 1991 Gulf crisis have also been studied: since oil ceased to arrive at the Dörtyol terminal, the whole industrial activity of that region has been impacted. The model will be used to select scenarios, priority actions and guidelines for integrated management.

The Plan will specify actions to remedy present pollution and to prevent further pollution in the whole İskenderun Gulf area: in the hinterland, in the coastal areas or in sea waters. Practical implementation measures will be largely dependent on the scenarios and priority actions to be chosen.

The "İskenderun project" includes in particular implementation measures relative to nature conservation. Natural sites are identified and analysed, in accordance with their national and international importance. Conservation policies and management schemes are being developed for these sites. The Ceyhan and Seyhan deltas, as well as the Amanos mountains where indigenous plant species are many and where the Belen Pass is used by numerous migratory birds, are among them.

The "İskenderun project" is part of a set of Mediterranean model projects which also concern Izmir, for instance, developed under the auspices of the UNEP Mediterranean Action Plan.

A strategy for financing should therefore consist of the following elements:

-- A combination of loans and grants from central government to municipalities for financing sewerage. Loans and the cost of operation and maintenance should be financed from sewerage charges imposed on the users;

-- A strict application of the Polluter-Pays-Principle for the river basins should be combined with use of pollution taxes to facilitate cross-subsidisation in the industrial sector and to prevent the immediate closure of a number of old industries;

-- The generation of funds for pollution control from development taxes on new industrial and tourist establishments (receipts could be paid into a special environment/conservation fund);

-- The abolition of the exemptions from local taxes or charges for business enterprises of any kind (tax revenues and charges could be used for environmental infrastructure and the provision of proper solid waste disposal);

-- The discontinuation of soft or low interest loans for the establishment of various types of enterprises (no low interest loans should be provided for secondary housing);

-- The application of water and sewerage charges to secondary residences on a flat-rate basis and corresponding to the average rate for houses with continuous occupancy;

-- The imposition of a special conservation tax on capital gains from the sale of all secondary housing (again, this should be paid into a special environment/conservation fund);

-- The sourcing of capital for the provision of water and sewerage services through the developers of housing estates or large tourist establishments;

-- The funding of major environmental infrastructures from international lending agencies.

5. *Compliance with international obligations*

Compliance with international obligations should be part of the overall implementation of strategy. This should include:

-- Compliance with the various international agreements already signed by Turkey concerning pollution of coastal water and the sea;

-- Special measures for highly endangered areas, such as the Black Sea.

In these efforts, the Turkish government should use the various international mechanisms and other types of technical assistance at its disposal. The government should also actively urge its neighbours to participate in collaborative efforts to solve common problems.

PROTECTION OF THE ENVIRONMENT IN THE BLACK SEA

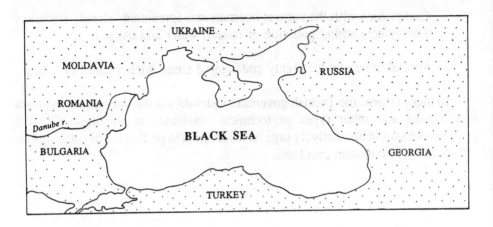

The Black Sea and its ecology

The Black Sea is a semi-enclosed sea with a surface area of 420 000 km². The Turkish Black Sea coast stretches for about 1 695 kms; about seven million people live on this coastal stretch, of which 40 per cent is urban. There are now seven coastal states; some of them are highly urbanised and industrialised, and all are employing intensive agricultural practices. The Sea has an indispensable value for the peoples of the coastal states, economically, socially and culturally.

The ecological and hydrological conditions of the Sea are quite specific and its flora and fauna are very sensitive to the changes in the composition and temperature of the sea water. Ninety per cent of the Black Sea basin is anoxic (lacking oxygen) and this level rises continuously, particularly in the middle parts of the basin, due to an increasing flux of organic matter.

The sea receives large quantities of domestic and industrial wastewater in untreated forms. Major pollution sources are rivers flowing into the sea, especially in the northwestern region. The amount transferred by the Bosphorus is unknown, but contribution to pollution by Turkish rivers is undoubtedly less than from the northwestern region.

The state of the environment in the marine and coastal areas of this delicate ecosystem became worse during the last few decades, owing to a dramatic increase in economic activities in the region as well as in continental Europe and Asia. The Black Sea states have a great interest in the protection of the marine environment and coastal areas against adverse environmental effects, and in conservation and sustainable development of natural resources and amenities.

Each coastal state implements some of its environmental measures in its coastal areas but these are clearly insufficient to correct the degradation of the Black Sea. International action is urgently required to overcome the pollution problem.

International measures for restoration of the Black Sea

The coastal states have made an attempt in this direction by negotiating a draft convention for environmental protection in the Black Sea. Negotiations started in 1988 and yielded the draft Convention for the Protection of the Black Sea Against Pollution and Three Protocols: Protocol for the Protection of the Black Sea Environment Against Pollution from Land-Based Sources, Protocol for the Protection of the Black Sea Environment from Pollution Due to Dumping, and Protocol Concerning Co-operation in Combating the Pollution of the Black Sea Marine Environment by Oil and Other Hazardous Substances in Emergency Situations. Although the text of the Convention was completed, it was not opened for signature in 1991. This Convention would provide a vital mechanism in matters pertaining to the Black Sea, and its Commission could serve as an intergovernmental body addressing the environmental problems in the region. The government of Turkey believes that riparian countries should sign this Convention as soon as possible and ensure that the Convention becomes a viable mechanism.

In order to accelerate action, the government of Turkey has commenced an initiative for starting a regional environment project in the Black Sea with the participation of all riparian countries. The proposal to initiate such a project was conveyed to the Executive Committee of the Global Environment Facility (GEF). This proposal has received support from various countries including the coastal ones and international organisations. Recently the GEF Executive Committee approved the proposal unanimously. The project will start as soon as the donors of the Facility endorse it. The proposed project includes preparatory work on the determination of the degree of environmental pollution and degradation. It will also assess the institutional, administrative, scientific, technical, technological and methodological needs for an effective and practical management programme and identify priority investment needs for the protection of the environment in the Black Sea's marine and coastal areas. Members of the Executive Committee, namely the United Nations Environment Programme, the United Nations Development Programme and the World Bank, are working with the national authorities of the coastal countries to prepare the project.

Assessment of progress

Progress on the restoration of the Black Sea has been very limited so far. With the exception of Turkey, the economic conditions in the coastal states restrict the authorities from taking major anti-pollution measures to limit the inflow of pollutants. Turkey is taking measures to limit the degradation of its coastal waters, but clearly urgent international actions with effective technical and financial assistance are needed to rescue the Black Sea. Among these actions OECD countries can assist through co-operative reduction of pollution input into the Danube river.

Together, the Convention and the proposed project, if urgently implemented, will make possible a response to environmental threats that jeopardise public health as well as the natural marine and coastal resources which are of great economic and social value to the countries of the region.

Chapter 5

GENERAL CONCLUSIONS

Turkey is in a stage of rapid and dynamic change and confronted with the **challenge of reconciling environment and unprecedented development**. Population growth is very high (24.3 per cent since 1980 compared to an OECD average of 6.7 per cent) and accompanied by largely uncontrolled urban growth. Its expanding and short-term-oriented economy (68.2 per cent rise in GDP since 1980, 66 per cent inflation for 1991) is undergoing major restructuring in industry, transport, energy, agriculture and tourism. These trends generate pollution and accentuate pressures on natural resources. Together with international issues (concerning, for instance, water resources, the Black Sea or international movements of wastes) they increasingly push environmental protection and its relation to development towards the top of the country's agenda.

In the past few years, significant **steps** have been **taken towards environmental progress**. A number of legislative and regulatory measures concerning the environment have been adopted; major development projects concerning water resources have been designed and launched; investments in sanitation and waste water treatment facilities have started; public transport has been reinforced as the major urban transport mode; natural gas has started being substituted for dirty fuels; some rehabilitation of inner cities has been carried out; and an Environment Ministry was created in 1991.

The OECD review of environmental policies in Turkey suggests improvements in two main directions to face the challenge fully and foster both environmental progress and sustainable development in the country. These are:

-- **integrating** environmental concerns in all appropriate sectors of economic activity and in all relevant governmental policies;

--   **implementing** environmental laws and policies effectively, including related institutional and financing changes.

General conclusions concerning integration and implementation are presented here. They are based on the more detailed conclusions concerning the management of water resources, urban pollution and the management of coastal zones, which bring together all the major issues policy-makers are confronted with today. Although these conclusions are specific to Turkey, they also reflect the essential elements of sound environmental policy throughout OECD countries: reducing the pollution burden, integrating environmental and economic decision-making, managing natural resources and strengthening international co-operation with respect to environmental issues.

I.   INTEGRATION OF ECONOMIC AND ENVIRONMENTAL POLICIES

Turkey is a highly centralised country and government is heavily involved in all aspects of economic life. While this centralisation is designed largely to promote economic growth and to provide an economic infrastructure for it, it is not sufficient in itself to ensure a sustainable development. Turkey has commenced to liberalise its economy and to give market forces a much greater role. This liberalisation calls attention however to the need to integrate economic and environmental policies. As the role of the state in planning declines with the growth of private sector activities, the role of the state in planning infrastructure and providing "public goods" including environmental services will increase; this in turn will require an even greater degree of co-ordination of policies and actions.

The assessment carried out in this review concludes that **integration of economic and environmental policies could reduce economic and environmental losses today and provide preventive policies for the future**. First, many laws, regulations, fiscal and other measures are in force to direct the economy and protect the environment; they are often not well co-ordinated and in some cases are contradictory. Second, integration of economic and environmental policies could apply to the formulation of policy objectives by highlighting the potential consequences of various sets of objectives. For example the relentless pursuit of tourism growth, in coastal areas, will be quickly negated by conflicts with industrial development and by environmental degradation. Third, integration at programme and project levels could highlight and minimise trade-offs between economic gains and environmental losses. For instance, by changing agricultural practices groundwater pollution could be

156

avoided without loss to production. Fourth, sustainable development can be achieved only if short- and long-term actions are integrated. For instance, the long-term demand for environmental and natural resources (water, forest, soil, marine resources) should be examined in a comprehensive way given their present and projected rates of use and consumption. Fifth, preventive environmental policies cannot be put into effect without a high degree of integration. As the relative cost/benefit effectiveness of preventive policies is high, policy integration would be a very cost-effective way of protecting the environment.

1.   *State commitment*

At the strategic level, the government has the opportunity to demonstrate its stated commitment to sustainable development by taking a number of new initiatives in integrating economic and environmental decision-making.

One way to do this would be to adopt formally a number of explicit environmental policy principles and concrete **environmental policy objectives** as part of a sustainable development strategy, possibly in the framework of a **"White Paper on Environmental Strategy"** which would outline within a minimum ten years' perspective the general principles and approaches to be adopted. The preparation of the White Paper would be undertaken jointly by the Ministry of Environment and the State Planning Organisation in consultation with all the other ministries concerned. Such a document would provide guidance to all ministries and departments for the interpretation of the government's intentions. The State Planning Organisation in its work on the five-year Development Plan and its evaluation of investment proposals could also use the White Paper.

Specific elements of this White Paper, within a minimum of ten years' perspective, could be:

-- strategic planning, especially concerning land use;

-- project planning, such as for the southeastern Anatolia project;

-- specific recommendations to state-owned enterprises;

-- international action in particular with regard to the Mediterranean, the Black Sea and water resources in the region.

157

2.   *Mechanisms for reconciliation of policy objectives and for integration of decision-making*

A high-level policy document such as proposed in the previous section will not, in itself, be sufficient to achieve the desired integration of economic and environmental decision-making. Integrative mechanisms must also be established at all levels of government, as suggested below.

Integration at Cabinet level

It is important to reconcile the environmental implications of economic development policies and, conversely, the economic consequences of environmental policies at Cabinet level. One option to achieve this would be the creation of an environment/resource management Cabinet Committee on which all development and economic ministers, as well as the Minister of Environment, would be represented. The Committee would review all economic development and environmental Cabinet papers. It would have the advantage of providing a single forum in which all environment/economy issues could be considered. Another option would be to make the **Environment Minister systematically a member of all economic development Cabinet Committees**. This would contribute better to the integration of environmental concerns in individual policy sectors such as energy, transport, tourism, industry and agriculture.

A separate measure that the government might wish to consider is to strengthen the role of the **Environment Council**. The membership of the Council could be formalised on a statutory basis as consisting of representatives of environmental groups, the relevant scientific or academic institutions, business, trade unions and government departments. The main responsibility of the Council would be to review policy objectives and advise the government on the integration of these objectives from the environmental viewpoint. The representatives of government departments in the Council would be there to listen and explain but would leave it to the other members to take the leading role.

Integration at departmental level

The role of the **Ministry of Environment** is clearly crucial in all aspects of environmental policy including integration. Changes needed to allow the ministry to fulfill its integration role will also probably equip it to carry out efficiently all its other roles, such as policy formulation and implementation. The

Ministry of Environment needs to be strengthened with economic and other appropriate expertise to fulfill the many facets of its integration role:

--   evaluating the economic impacts of environmental policies and the impacts of economic policies on the environment;

--   maintaining specific links with the State Planning Organisation and the State Institute of Statistics, including participation in the planning process at various levels;

--   maintaining links with the various economic ministries;

--   providing support for the inter-departmental committees.

It also needs to face expanding international responsibilities such as negotiating agreements, monitoring their implementation and participating in international work in general.

The State Planning Organisation (SPO) has an equally important integration role as it prepares five-year development plans and decides on investment priorities based on the investment requirements submitted to it by the various spending departments. To ensure better integration within this planning process, it is suggested that environmental expertise be strengthened and placed within SPO where it can influence analysis and decisions best. As the only agency that can lay down evaluation requirements for investment, the SPO has the power to require that environmental considerations be incorporated into the investment proposals, totally or partially financed from public funds, and to judge whether this has been done. It would be advisable that links between the SPO and Ministry of Environment ensure that environmental considerations are integrated into major government investment proposals and that related decisions are taken on the basis of an integrated evaluation. An environmental assessment should be done for all sectoral projects and programmes.

Other government departments, including the various development and economic ministries, will also have specific environmental briefs derived from the objectives specified for their respective domains in the White Paper. It will also be necessary to make environmental information respond better to decision-making needs.

The White Paper should also provide common ground for officials of the Ministry of Environment and other ministries to co-operate systematically at administrative level in **standing or ad hoc inter-departmental committees.**

Committees of this type already exist. The position of lead agency would depend on the issue at hand, but at all times the lead agency should take account of the views of the other departments. Differences that cannot be resolved at administrative level should be identified and referred to the political decision-makers. The inter-departmental committees described here are not the same as the existing Supreme Environment Board, which is a top-level body. Rather, they would be involved in the day-to-day policy formulation processes of government, comprising the personnel actually dealing with the various issues in the different departments.

Integration at provincial level

Policies are implemented at the provincial level either by a combination of the different metropolitan and district municipalities and central government agencies or by central agencies alone. Turkey being a highly centralised country, there is a strong presence in all provinces of all major government ministries. The governor of each province, under the Ministry of the Interior, is responsible for co-ordination between municipalities and governmental agencies and for ensuring that policies are implemented according to the policy guidelines of the government. This leaves the governor considerable freedom in integrating policies.

Because the governor's position is already one of integrating different aspects of government policy, it is well suited to deal with environmental issues as well. However, integration could be considerably improved if the **governor's office** had a fuller understanding of the benefits of preventive environmental policies and of the necessity of integration to realise these benefits. This would require special training or appointment of an official to the governor's office with the appropriate understanding of environment policies and integration.

Laws 3030 and 3194 set down specific guidelines for co-ordinating various activities (investment in infrastructure and transport) in metropolitan and other municipalities and the relationship between central and municipal government. These laws have been in operation for a number of years and their operational effectiveness should be examined in terms of environmental integration.

Integration among municipalities, separated by areas under the direct control of the governor, is difficult, as in most cases no specific mechanisms exist for formal co-operation. In certain coastal areas, for example, this leads to over-development and environmental degradation. It is suggested that associations of district municipalities be fostered, that their development be integrated and that preventive policies be put in place.

II.   IMPLEMENTATION

To face its environmental challenge, the second main direction lies in a systematic, large-scale implementation effort to translate the environmental policies into daily environmental management improvements and related economic and social benefits. Innovative and determined actions will be needed concerning environmental institutions, mechanisms of implementation and financing.

1.   *Institutional changes*

Looking at the experiences of OECD countries, it is evident that national governments have responded to their environmental needs in a variety of institutional ways. Certain governments have established major departments of environment embracing responsibilities not only for policy, co-ordination and research, but also for the management of environmental resources such as water, air, and land. Environmental protection, and the management of certain major sectors of government related to the environment, such as health, housing and transport and even regional government, have also formed part of their responsibilities. Other governments simply extended existing ministries or established new ones for policy planning and co-ordination, but without any programme management functions. In between, a variety of structures have developed. Similarly, the relationships between national government and other tiers of government vary widely.

Ministry of Environment

Three options for institutional change are suggested below for consideration by the Turkish authorities. (Table 12) The options are formulated in such a way as to give a differing emphasis to each of the following elements identified previously in this report:

--   maintain the positive features of the current institutional
        framework in Turkey;

161

Table 12. OPTIONS FOR INSTITUTIONAL CHANGE

1 **Status Quo Plus**	2 **Integrated Management + Deconcentration**	3 **Integrated Management + Local Decision-Making**
Strengthen enforcement capability of Dept. of Health, State Hydraulic Works and integration capability of State Planning Organisation	Transfer regulatory and enforcement powers to Ministry of Environment; strengthen integration capability of State Planning Organisation	Transfer regulatory powers to Ministry of Environment, and enforcement to Regional Environment Agencies; strengthen integration capability of State Planning Organisation
Expand resourcing of Ministry of Environment Head Office	Head Office of the Ministry of Environment responsible for: - legislation - formulating national regulations and standards - integrating economic/environment policies - research	Head Office of the Ministry of Environment responsible for: As in Option 2
Begin establishment of Regional Directorates of the Ministry of Environment Provide environmental expertise in Governor's Office	Regional Directorates of the Ministry of Environment responsible for: - enforcement of regulations and standards - administration of charges and subsidies - monitoring & resource inventories - indicative planning for integrated river basin management and coastal zone management - advice to Governor & co-ordination between central government and municipal agencies - demand management, auditing EIAs, etc.	Regional Directorates of the Ministry of Environment responsible for: - co-ordination of central govt. activities in regions - advice to Governor's Office - overseeing of Regional Environment Agencies Regional Environment Agencies responsible for: - enforcement of regulations and standards - administration of charges and subsidies - monitoring & resource inventories - indicative planning for integrated river basin management and coastal zone management - demand management, auditing EIAs, etc.
Coastal Zone Management Councils: Co-ordination of all development and environmental factors	Coastal Zone Management Councils: As in Option 1	Coastal Zone Management Councils: As in Option 1
Municipalities responsible for: land use planning, delivery of water services, municipal waste management, noise control	Municipalities responsible for: As in Option 1	Municipalities responsible for: As in Option 1

162

--   establish an institutional framework that encourages integration of different policy areas;

--   acknowledge the Turkish government's move to further deconcentration, in other words, to take the environmental central administration closer to "the field";

--   bring about a greater decentralisation, in other words, a greater involvement of the local people and authorities in environmental administration.

The options are **not mutually exclusive**, but rather reflect stages in a possible institutional evolution.

The first option is one of minimum change, or "Status Quo Plus" and therefore feasible in the short term.   At present, Turkey has the type of institutional arrangement where the regulatory functions are placed with various ministries while the Ministry of Environment has only policy, planning and co-ordinating functions. This option would leave these arrangements in place, but would require provision of additional resources to ensure that environmental functions, especially enforcement functions, could be carried out more effectively.

This report has already pointed out the disadvantages of giving regulatory functions to administrations each of which has a differing or even a conflicting focus.   One example has been presented in the chapter on water resource management.   There is a clear conflict at present in the development and economic ministries between their role as developers and their role as protectors of the environment. Given their long tradition as resource developers and the pressure in Turkey to achieve a high rate of development, they tend to subordinate their environmental responsibilities to these other roles. The present allocation of environmental responsibilities could thus lead to further deterioration in the environment and the resource base.

The second option for institutional change emphasises the integration theme by stressing the transfer of regulatory and enforcement functions now held by the General Directorate of State Hydraulic Works and the Ministry of Health to the Ministry of Environment. This option also stresses deconcentration by assigning many of the responsibilities to Regional Directorates of the Ministry of Environment, which would have to be resourced adequately in order to realise the proposed changes.   The words "region" and "regional" are used in this chapter to indicate an area on the scale of a major river basin.   The proposed division of functions between the Ministry's Head Office and its Regional

Directorates assigns policy and nationwide issues to Head Office, while area-specific and operational issues (enforcement, administration of pollution charges, the formulation of river basin management plans, coastal resource inventories, etc.) would become the task of the Regional Directorates.

The third option for institutional change adds the element of local participation in environmental management by proposing a new type of organisation which could be called Regional Environment Agencies. These would be regionally funded, and would include on their boards elected local officials and representatives of enterprises, and other non-governmental organisations; they would therefore have a certain independence from central government. The Regional Environment Agencies would carry out most of the functions assigned to the Regional Directorates of the Ministry of Environment under option two, leaving these Regional Directorates with more of an advisory and co-ordinating role amongst the regional offices of central government agencies.

The Regional Environment Agencies in this third option would be, from the citizen's point of view, the most visible of the environmental agencies: they would handle discharge and emission permits, administer pollution charges and provide subsidies for treatment stations, and formulate river basin management plans and indicative plans for coastal zone management. The Agencies would also have to implement national policies and standards decided on by central government through the Ministry of Environment.

Coastal Zone Management Councils (CZMCs) and Municipalities

CZMCs are proposed here to deal with the special problems of coastal zones where the intense pressure of competing demands creates the need for some special provision to ensure the integration of decision-making. CZMCs would be co-ordinating councils and would bring together representatives of all the central and municipal agencies with an interest in a particular coastal area. To work more efficiently and expeditiously, they would be serviced by a small secretariat, with the major work being done by the relevant agencies.

Two areas have been identified where **municipalities** should be given additional responsibilities:

> -- In coastal zones without a CZMC, several municipalities should form associations or unions to co-ordinate the overall development of their combined areas including areas within their

boundaries and those situated between their boundaries and which are presently under the authority of the governors. Such associations already exist and others could be formed informally or on a statutory basis;

-- There is a conflict at the municipal level between the role of the municipalities as polluters through their sewerage systems and their role as enforcers of environmental legislation. These two roles need to be separated by making water and sewage companies independent and/or by giving the regulatory powers to the Ministry of Environment or the Regional Environment Agency.

2. *Mechanisms of implementation*

Turkey already has in place many of the elements required for the efficient implementation of agreed policies, regulations and standards. For example, there is already a set of legislative measures that fully recognise the main principles for environmental management. In some other areas, there is a need to strengthen existing practices if these are to meet the challenges of the future, and Turkish authorities might wish to consider the following suggestions.

Implementation of regulations and standards

A prerequisite to enforcement of regulations and standards is their clear definition, and their specification in a way amenable to monitoring and enforcement. Their responsibilities for the **enforcement of regulations** are most effectively carried out if these are assigned to an agency which has a clearly defined enforcement role that is not contradicted by any of its other functions. Such an agency should be required by law to give account of its performance to the government and the public at large; funding of its enforcement activities should be done largely by the users.

Complementary measures for the implementation of policies such as the **greater use of economic instruments** could be considered jointly by officials from relevant ministries: environment, finance, transport, industry, trade, agriculture, etc. Some specific recommendations for the use of economic instruments have already been made in this report, but could be considered for a whole range of issues:

--   pollution charges on industrial wastewater discharges;

--   resource pricing for irrigation water;

--   subsidies for soil conservation activities;

--   deposit refund systems for various recyclable materials such as car batteries;

--   enforcement incentives such as performance bonds.

Environmental impact assessment

As a matter of urgency the environmental impact assessment law should be implemented. To assist implementation clear guidance needs to be provided as to the range of activities to be subject to environmental impact assessment; they would have to include all major industrial, energy and tourism developments as well as land-use changes involving substantial areas of land.

Emphasis on demand management

Integrated resource management requires that supply management be balanced with demand management. There is considerable scope for more emphasis on demand management aspects in the use of water and electricity, especially in terms of the application of economic instruments.

Environmental information

Information plays a vital role in all stages of the environmental management process. Resource inventories are required in order to formulate standards; monitoring of emissions and discharges will show whether permit conditions are being met; monitoring of ambient conditions (air pollution, water quality, etc.) will show the state of the environment. The management, use and dissemination of environmental information needs to be an important function of the Ministry of Environment and therefore requires proper funding. The State Institute of Statistics already plays a role in the provision of environmental information and this role should be expanded, particularly for data coming from surveys, census and remote sensing. The fact that it also collects standard socio-economic information further places the Institute in an excellent position to contribute co-ordinated information to the formulation of the sustainable development policies of the Turkish government in general, and to strategic planners in the State Planning Organisation in particular. The establishment of an integrated environmental information system should be given priority.

Public participation

The 1987 Brundtland Commission report "Our Common Future" emphasized the importance of public participation in achieving sustainable development. Even the most enlightened government policies will fail if they are not supported by a public which endorses their objectives and participates in their implementation.

Mechanisms for public participation need to be present at different levels. It is important for citizens to have a voice at the project level. Permit and consent procedures involved in physical planning and in the protection of water and air quality also need to be open and easily accessible to the public without undue cost or legal obstacles.

The democratic nations of OECD rely heavily on public participation and in most of them today environmental policy is driven by public demand. Here the constructive role of the environmental non-governmental organisations (NGOs) should be recognised by inviting them to participate more closely in the policy formulation process. At all levels or in all areas the government can assist in developing public participation by providing relevant and timely information to the public.

Protection of special areas

Protection of special areas requires stricter standards and/or specific measures to protect, for example, fragile and/or highly valuable ecological systems; these regions include coastal areas, wetlands, cultural and archaeological sites. Present protection of these areas needs to be reinforced and protection measures should override touristic and other types of development. More detailed recommendations on the implementation of policies have been made in previous chapters and are not repeated here.

State enterprise sector

The state enterprise sector represents a significant part of the Turkish economy. This sector needs to be subject to the same degree of enforcement of environmental regulations and standards as the private sector. In fact, the Turkish government has a unique opportunity to lead by example and implement integrated pollution management policies, install clean technologies in the enterprises it owns, or relocate or close them down.

3. *Financing*

Financing of environmental measures in both the public and private sectors will depend on the type of financing instruments used, on the determination of the government to raise sufficient funds and the ability of the economy to generate funds. The higher economic growth is, the greater that ability will be.

The financing strategy for environmental purposes could be based on the following main sources:

-- governmental financing, consisting of revenues from central government, local government revenues, charges raised on publicly-provided services, other environmentally related revenues and eco-taxes;

-- financing by industry of its own pollution expenditures, and public/private partnerships to finance environmental infrastructure projects;

-- international financing, particularly from international lending institutions.

Governmental financing

The government should aim at **reducing future financing requirements** to a minimum by putting maximum **emphasis on preventive policies** in industrial investment, energy production and use, in transport policy and in resource development and use. For each sector, a specific strategy needs to be developed with the aim of preventing pollution growth and resource waste. A start has already been made in some areas. The use of natural gas in some urban areas has significantly reduced pollution, and the associated cost is relatively low and largely borne by the individual householders who benefit from cleaner air. Similarly, strategies to develop public transport in major metropolitan areas will produce environmental benefits. Such strategy must include the enforcement of pollution control investment and the introduction of low-polluting production technologies in new industrial plants. Part of this strategy will also shift the burden of financing to the private sector.

The backlog in publicly-provided environmental services, such as water and sewerage systems and solid waste collection treatment and disposal, is considerable and the need is especially urgent since public health is endangered and serious damage has been caused to water resources and coastal waters. The main source of financing for these services should be **user charges**, preferably calculated on the basis of the **long-run full social cost** of providing them. These costs should also take into account: the cost of resource depletion, the environment costs associated with the provision of the services, and the high rate of inflation in Turkey. Although the government should aim for the full recovery of capital and running costs, there will be circumstances where for reasons of equity they cannot be fully recouped and have to be financed from taxes. In a number of cases, developers can be obliged to provide sewerage and water services as a condition of their obtaining a development permit. Such a policy would relieve the government of the burden of financing these developments and could be applied to tourism development areas, secondary housing or major suburban developments. The management aspect of financing publicly provided services would be a joint effort by central and local governments.

The government could raise **additional funds for environment** by imposing **development taxes** on land in cases in which building permits provide windfall profits to industrial or commercial developers and to housing or hotel developers in the tourism sector. These taxes could be tied to performance in fulfilling environmental requirements and could be largely raised by local governments. Additional public funds could be made available by **transferring subsidies** presently granted to developers in tourism, industry and commerce to the provision of these public services. In general, the present subsidy policy for industrial and tourism development and for many government enterprises is of dubious economic value and is environmentally damaging. These funds could be used for providing environmental infrastructure with little or no loss to the economy.

Penalties and fees for non-compliance should be more strictly enforced than at present and could remain in full with the municipalities which are imposing them. They should be spent on public treatment installations.

169

Product charges could be imposed on certain polluting products, both to reduce their use and to generate funds for waste disposal and treatment. Similarly, **deposit refund** schemes and **performance bonds** would produce revenues in case of non-performance such as disposal of hazardous waste or surface mining.

Financing of pollution control by industry

A significant proportion of industry in Turkey is state-owned; some of it is old, inefficient and highly polluting. Part of this industry is in densely populated areas; its pollution therefore impacts on large numbers of people. Some of this industry will have to be retrofitted and subsidised; however, many plants will have to be closed soon for both economic and environmental reasons instead of being retrofitted. Financing for pollution control subsidies could come from **effluent charges** imposed on all plants in a given river basin or airshed.

Although subsidisation of the development of new technology itself is often necessary, no subsidy should be provided for investments in **new plants**, for pollution prevention and control either in the public or in the private sector. The Environment Law of 1983 should be enforced and this should lead both domestic and foreign investors to use the latest low-polluting technologies, which are normally the most profitable ones. **Differentiated taxation** of polluting fuels would also provide additional revenues and at the same time discourage the use of the most polluting fuels.

Large investment projects could be jointly financed through **public/private partnerships**. The private sector would provide the investment funds and running costs in return for collecting revenues for a limited period after which the infrastructure would be returned to public ownership. Alternatives are privatisation of certain public services with strict governmental controls over price and quality provided. These can include water, sewerage, waste disposal and conservation services.

International financing

For development purposes, all sectors of the Turkish economy will depend on foreign investment for some years to come. Investment for environmental purposes could also be financed from foreign sources. Criteria of "economic viability" or "ability to raise foreign exchange" from environmental investment can be met in many cases if the appropriate investment analysis is employed over a sufficiently long period. The evaluation of the Izmir sewerage system is one example. The Turkish authorities could make full use of the funds that would be available from international and national development aid or lending institutions. They should also challenge these institutions to demonstrate in Turkey that "clean, green" economic growth (e.g. in industrialisation and energy development) is possible. Conversely, this aid is and could increasingly be made conditional on an environmental impact analysis of the project concerned.

OECD Member governments could assist Turkey's environmental progress by encouraging their own multinationals operating there to put into practice the environmental regulations in effect in their countries of origin.

Conditions for financing

Various conditions have to be complied with if the funding mechanisms suggested above are to operate successfully:

-- the large capital expenditures, such as sewerage and water treatment, will have to be financed through credits, and it is the responsibility of the central and local government to raise these funds from either internal or international sources. These credits can then be recouped through proper pricing and charging. Although Turkey will be facing considerable budgetary difficulties for some time in the future, this should not be used as an excuse to delay such investments;

-- funds raised through economic instruments in the field of pollution control or conservation and also from certain taxes, such as fuel taxes, might either be earmarked and paid into a special environmental fund, or retained by the municipalities raising them in order to finance their environmental services;

-- subsidies for pollution control should be used only in conformity with the PPP; subsidies presently provided for industry and tourism, which distort prices and the market in general (such as subsidies for tourism development or to polluting industries), should be diverted to finance public environmental expenditures.

LIST OF THE MEMBERS OF THE OECD REVIEW TEAM

NATIONAL EXPERTS

Mr. W. BARCHARD	(Canada)
Mr. R. BAUMAN	(USA)
Ms. S. BOROVNICA	(Yugoslavia)
Mr. P. BROWNE-COOPER	(Australia)
Mr. G. COGLIANDRO	(Italy)
Mr. F. GIGLIANI	(Italy)
Mr. E. GOLDBERG	(New Zealand)
Mr. V. RANTA-PERE	(Finland)
Mr. F. WERRING	(Netherlands)

OECD SECRETARIAT

Mr. C. AVÉROUS
Mr. M. POTIER

Consultants

Mr. F. JUHASZ	(Australia)
Ms. C. KUZUCUOGLU	(France)
Ms. E. LEVIEUX	(USA)
Mr. H.H. YILDIRIM	(Turkey)

MAIN SALES OUTLETS OF OECD PUBLICATIONS
PRINCIPAUX POINTS DE VENTE DES PUBLICATIONS DE L'OCDE

ARGENTINA – ARGENTINE
Carlos Hirsch S.R.L.
Galería Güemes, Florida 165, 4° Piso
1333 Buenos Aires   Tel. (1) 331.1787 y 331.2391
Telefax: (1) 331.1787

AUSTRALIA – AUSTRALIE
D.A. Book (Aust.) Pty. Ltd.
648 Whitehorse Road, P.O.B 163
Mitcham, Victoria 3132   Tel. (03) 873.4411
Telefax: (03) 873.5679

AUSTRIA – AUTRICHE
Gerold & Co.
Graben 31
Wien I   Tel. (0222) 533.50.14

BELGIUM – BELGIQUE
Jean De Lannoy
Avenue du Roi 202
B-1060 Bruxelles   Tel. (02) 538.51.69/538.08.41
Telefax: (02) 538.08.41

CANADA
Renouf Publishing Company Ltd.
1294 Algoma Road
Ottawa, ON K1B 3W8   Tel. (613) 741.4333
Telefax: (613) 741.5439
Stores:
61 Sparks Street
Ottawa, ON K1P 5R1   Tel. (613) 238.8985
211 Yonge Street
Toronto, ON M5B 1M4   Tel. (416) 363.3171
Les Éditions La Liberté Inc.
3020 Chemin Sainte-Foy
Sainte-Foy, PQ G1X 3V6   Tel. (418) 658.3763
Telefax: (418) 658.3763

Federal Publications
165 University Avenue
Toronto, ON M5H 3B8   Tel. (416) 581.1552
Telefax: (416) 581.1743

CHINA – CHINE
China National Publications Import
Export Corporation (CNPIEC)
P.O. Box 88
Beijing   Tel. 403.5533
Telefax: 401.5664

DENMARK – DANEMARK
Munksgaard Export and Subscription Service
35, Nørre Søgade, P.O. Box 2148
DK-1016 København K   Tel. (33) 12.85.70
Telefax: (33) 12.93.87

FINLAND – FINLANDE
Akateeminen Kirjakauppa
Keskuskatu 1, P.O. Box 128
00100 Helsinki   Tel. (358 0) 12141
Telefax: (358 0) 121.4441

FRANCE
OECD/OCDE
Mail Orders/Commandes par correspondance:
2, rue André-Pascal
75775 Paris Cedex 16   Tel. (33-1) 45.24.82.00
Telefax: (33-1) 45.24.85.00   or (33-1) 45.24.81.76
Telex: 620 160 OCDE
OECD Bookshop/Librairie de l'OCDE :
33, rue Octave-Feuillet
75016 Paris   Tel. (33-1) 45.24.81.67
(33-1) 45.24.81.81
Documentation Française
29, quai Voltaire
75007 Paris   Tel. 40.15.70.00
Gibert Jeune (Droit-Économie)
6, place Saint-Michel
75006 Paris   Tel. 43.25.91.19

Librairie du Commerce International
10, avenue d'Iéna
75016 Paris   Tel. 40.73.34.60
Librairie Dunod
Université Paris-Dauphine
Place du Maréchal de Lattre de Tassigny
75016 Paris   Tel. 47.27.18.56
Librairie Lavoisier
11, rue Lavoisier
75008 Paris   Tel. 42.65.39.95
Librairie L.G.D.J. - Montchrestien
20, rue Soufflot
75005 Paris   Tel. 46.33.89.85
Librairie des Sciences Politiques
30, rue Saint-Guillaume
75007 Paris   Tel. 45.48.36.02
P.U.F.
49, boulevard Saint-Michel
75005 Paris   Tel. 43.25.83.40
Librairie de l'Université
12a, rue Nazareth
13100 Aix-en-Provence   Tel. (16) 42.26.18.08
Documentation Française
165, rue Garibaldi
69003 Lyon   Tel. (16) 78.63.32.23

GERMANY – ALLEMAGNE
OECD Publications and Information Centre
Schedestrasse 7
D-W 5300 Bonn 1   Tel. (0228) 21.60.45
Telefax: (0228) 26.11.04

GREECE – GRÈCE
Librairie Kauffmann
Mavrokordatou 9
106 78 Athens   Tel. 322.21.60
Telefax: 363.39.67

HONG-KONG
Swindon Book Co. Ltd.
13–15 Lock Road
Kowloon, Hong Kong   Tel. 366.80.31
Telefax: 739.49.75

ICELAND – ISLANDE
Mál Mog Menning
Laugavegi 18, Pósthólf 392
121 Reykjavik   Tel. 162.35.23

INDIA – INDE
Oxford Book and Stationery Co.
Scindia House
New Delhi 110001   Tel.(11) 331.5896/5308
Telefax: (11) 332.5993
17 Park Street
Calcutta 700016   Tel. 240832

INDONESIA – INDONÉSIE
Pdii-Lipi
P.O. Box 4298
Jakarta 12042   Tel. 583467
Telex: 62 875

IRELAND – IRLANDE
TDC Publishers – Library Suppliers
12 North Frederick Street
Dublin 1   Tel. 74.48.35/74.96.77
Telefax: 74.84.16

ISRAEL
Electronic Publications only
Publications électroniques seulement
Sophist Systems Ltd.
71 Allenby Street
Tel-Aviv 65134   Tel. 3-29.00.21
Telefax: 3-29.92.39

ITALY – ITALIE
Libreria Commissionaria Sansoni
Via Duca di Calabria 1/1
50125 Firenze   Tel. (055) 64.54.15
Telefax: (055) 64.12.57
Via Bartolini 29
20155 Milano   Tel. (02) 36.50.83
Editrice e Libreria Herder
Piazza Montecitorio 120
00186 Roma   Tel. 679.46.28
Telefax: 678.47.51
Libreria Hoepli
Via Hoepli 5
20121 Milano   Tel. (02) 86.54.46
Telefax: (02) 805.28.86
Libreria Scientifica
Dott. Lucio de Biasio 'Aeiou'
Via Coronelli, 6
20146 Milano   Tel. (02) 48.95.45.52
Telefax: (02) 48.95.45.48

JAPAN – JAPON
OECD Publications and Information Centre
Landic Akasaka Building
2-3-4 Akasaka, Minato-ku
Tokyo 107   Tel. (81.3) 3586.2016
Telefax: (81.3) 3584.7929

KOREA – CORÉE
Kyobo Book Centre Co. Ltd.
P.O. Box 1658, Kwang Hwa Moon
Seoul   Tel. 730.78.91
Telefax: 735.00.30

MALAYSIA – MALAISIE
Co-operative Bookshop Ltd.
University of Malaya
P.O. Box 1127, Jalan Pantai Baru
59700 Kuala Lumpur
Malaysia   Tel. 756.5000/756.5425
Telefax: 755.4424

NETHERLANDS – PAYS-BAS
SDU Uitgeverij
Christoffel Plantijnstraat 2
Postbus 20014
2500 EA's-Gravenhage   Tel. (070 3) 78.99.11
Voor bestellingen: Tel. (070 3) 78.98.80
Telefax: (070 3) 47.63.51

NEW ZEALAND
NOUVELLE-ZÉLANDE
Legislation Services
P.O. Box 12418
Thorndon, Wellington   Tel. (04) 496.5652
Telefax: (04) 496.5698

NORWAY – NORVÈGE
Narvesen Info Center – NIC
Bertrand Narvesens vei 2
P.O. Box 6125 Etterstad
0602 Oslo 6   Tel. (02) 57.33.00
Telefax: (02) 68.19.01

PAKISTAN
Mirza Book Agency
65 Shahrah Quaid-E-Azam
Lahore 3   Tel. 66.839
Telex: 44886 UBL PK. Attn: MIRZA BK

PORTUGAL
Livraria Portugal
Rua do Carmo 70-74
Apart. 2681
1117 Lisboa Codex   Tel.: (01) 347.49.82/3/4/5
Telefax: (01) 347.02.64

SINGAPORE – SINGAPOUR
Information Publications Pte
Golden Wheel Bldg.
41, Kallang Pudding, #04-03
Singapore 1334   Tel. 741.5166
                                   Telefax: 742.9356

SPAIN – ESPAGNE
Mundi-Prensa Libros S.A.
Castelló 37, Apartado 1223
Madrid 28001   Tel. (91) 431.33.99
                                   Telefax: (91) 575.39.98

Libreria Internacional AEDOS
Consejo de Ciento 391
08009 – Barcelona   Tel. (93) 488.34.92
                                   Telefax: (93) 487.76.59
Llibreria de la Generalitat
Palau Moja
Rambla dels Estudis, 118
08002 – Barcelona
            (Subscripcions) Tel. (93) 318.80.12
            (Publicacions) Tel. (93) 302.67.23
                      Telefax: (93) 412.18.54

SRI LANKA
Centre for Policy Research
c/o Colombo Agencies Ltd.
No. 300-304, Galle Road
Colombo 3   Tel. (1) 574240, 573551-2
                      Telefax: (1) 575394, 510711

SWEDEN – SUÈDE
Fritzes Fackboksföretaget
Box 16356
Regeringsgatan 12
103 27 Stockholm   Tel. (08) 23.89.00
                                   Telefax: (08) 20.50.21

Subscription Agency-Agence d'abonnements
Wennergren-Williams AB
Nordenflychtsvägen 74
Box 30004
104 25 Stockholm   Tel. (08) 13.67.00
                                   Telefax: (08) 618.62.32

SWITZERLAND – SUISSE
Maditec S.A. (Books and Periodicals - Livres
et périodiques)
Chemin des Palettes 4
1020 Renens/Lausanne   Tel. (021) 635.08.65
                                   Telefax: (021) 635.07.80

Mail orders only - Commandes
par correspondance seulement
Librairie Payot
C.P. 3212
1002 Lausanne   Telefax: (021) 311.13.92

Librairie Unilivres
6, rue de Candolle
1205 Genève   Tel. (022) 320.26.23
                                   Telefax: (022) 329.73.18

Subscription Agency - Agence d'abonnement
Naville S.A.
38 avenue Vibert
1227 Carouge   Tél.: (022) 308.05.56/57
                      Telefax: (022) 308.05.88

See also – Voir aussi :
OECD Publications and Information Centre
Schedestrasse 7
D-W 5300 Bonn 1 (Germany)
                      Tel. (49.228) 21.60.45
                      Telefax: (49.228) 26.11.04

TAIWAN – FORMOSE
Good Faith Worldwide Int'l. Co. Ltd.
9th Floor, No. 118, Sec. 2
Chung Hsiao E. Road
Taipei   Tel. (02) 391.7396/391.7397
                      Telefax: (02) 394.9176

THAILAND – THAÏLANDE
Suksit Siam Co. Ltd.
113, 115 Fuang Nakhon Rd.
Opp. Wat Rajbopith
Bangkok 10200   Tel. (662) 251.1630
                                   Telefax: (662) 236.7783

TURKEY – TURQUIE
Kültur Yayinlari Is-Türk Ltd. Sti.
Atatürk Bulvari No. 191/Kat. 13
Kavaklidere/Ankara   Tel. 428.11.40 Ext. 2458
Dolmabahce Cad. No. 29
Besiktas/Istanbul   Tel. 160.71.88
                                   Telex: 43482B

UNITED KINGDOM – ROYAUME-UNI
HMSO
Gen. enquiries   Tel. (071) 873 0011
Postal orders only:
P.O. Box 276, London SW8 5DT
Personal Callers HMSO Bookshop
49 High Holborn, London WC1V 6HB
                      Telefax: (071) 873 8200
Branches at: Belfast, Birmingham, Bristol, Edin-
burgh, Manchester

UNITED STATES – ÉTATS-UNIS
OECD Publications and Information Centre
2001 L Street N.W., Suite 700
Washington, D.C. 20036-4910 Tel. (202) 785.6323
                      Telefax: (202) 785.0350

VENEZUELA
Libreria del Este
Avda F. Miranda 52, Aptdo. 60337
Edificio Galipán
Caracas 106   Tel. 951.1705/951.2307/951.1297
                 Telegram: Libreste Caracas

YUGOSLAVIA – YOUGOSLAVIE
Jugoslovenska Knjiga
Knez Mihajlova 2, P.O. Box 36
Beograd   Tel. (011) 621.992
                                   Telefax: (011) 625.970

Orders and inquiries from countries where Distribu-
tors have not yet been appointed should be sent to:
OECD Publications Service, 2 rue André-Pascal,
75775 Paris Cedex 16, France.

Les commandes provenant de pays où l'OCDE n'a
pas encore désigné de distributeur devraient être
adressées à : OCDE, Service des Publications,
2, rue André-Pascal, 75775 Paris Cedex 16, France.

Subscription to OECD periodicals may also be
placed through main subscription agencies.

Les abonnements aux publications périodiques de
l'OCDE peuvent être souscrits auprès des
principales agences d'abonnement.

OECD PUBLICATIONS, 2 rue André-Pascal, 75775 PARIS CEDEX 16
PRINTED IN FRANCE
(97 92 10 1) ISBN 92-64-13749-1 - No. 46103 1992